The State of Dependency:
Welfare Under Labour

THE SOCIAL MARKET FOUNDATION

The Foundation's main activity is to commission and publish original papers by independent academic and other experts on key topics in the economic and social fields, with a view to stimulating public discussion on the performance of markets and the social framework within which they operate.

The Foundation is a registered charity and a company limited by guarantee. It is independent of any political party or group and is financed by the sales of publications and by voluntary donations from individuals, organisations and companies.

The views expressed in its publications are those of the authors and do not represent a corporate opinion of the Foundation.

PATRONS
Viscount Chandos
Lord Flowers FRS
Rt Hon. Lord Owen CH
Lord Sainsbury

CHAIRMAN
Professor Lord Skidelsky FBA

MEMBERS OF THE ADVISORY COUNCIL
Professor Nick Bosanquet
Sir Samuel Brittan
Evan Davis
Michael Fallon MP
Liam Halligan
Professor John Kay
Lawrence Mone
Alex de Mont
Ian Pearson MP
Andrew Tyrie MP
David Willetts MP
John Willman

MEMBERS OF THE BOARD
Nick Alexander
Alex de Mont
Christopher Stone

DIRECTOR
Katharine Raymond

EDITORIAL CONSULTANT
Lord Kilmarnock

The State of Dependency:
Welfare Under Labour

The Social Market Foundation
March 2000

First published in English by The Social Market Foundation, 2000
in association with Profile Books Ltd

The Social Market Foundation
11 Tufton Street
London SW1P 3QB

Profile Books Ltd
58A Hatton Garden
London EC1N 8LX

Copyright © The Social Market Foundation 2000

The moral right of the author has been asserted.

All rights reserved. Without limiting the rights under copyright reserved above, no part of this publication may be reproduced, stored or introduced into a retrieval system, or transmitted, in any form or by any means (electronic, mechanical, photocopying, recording or otherwise), without the prior written permission of both the copyright owner and the publisher of this book.

Typeset in Bembo by MacGuru
macguru2@appleonline.net

Printed in Great Britain by Hobbs the Printers

A CIP catalogue record for this book is available from the British Library.

Paper No. 45

ISBN 1 874097 52 6

Contents

Acknowledgements		vii
Introduction		viii
1	The Route March to Welfare Reform	1
2	What Then Was Unthinkable?	34
3	The Eye Of The Storm	58
4	Welfare in the Age of Low Taxation	74
5	T. S. Eliot's View of Human Nature and the Debate on Welfare	90
6	Altruism, Self-Interest and the Sustainability of Welfare	98
7	The Role of Welfare in an Inclusive Society	116
8	Welfare: A Bird's Eye View	120
9	Its's The Economy, Stupid!	131
10	Two Contrary Views on Welfare Reform	144
11	A Year of Delivery	149
	Publications	169

For Jill Hendey

Acknowledgements

A number of people have actively supported the production of these essays. Damian Leeson and Ben Forsyth have read through the entire manuscript. Richard Cracknell, from the House of Commons Library, produced much of the statistical analysis underpinning the arguments that follow. Sara Lander, from the Social Market Foundation, has overseen the production of the paper. To each of these individuals I record my debt. But Jill Hendey has again produced the manuscript for publication. To her this book is dedicated as a small recognition of the ability she constantly shows as my secretary and for her friendship over more than 25 years.

Introduction

New Labour came to power committed to transform welfare. That revolutionary intent has fractured.

Thinking the unthinkable had been the task in Opposition. It was not an activity for Government. And, far from being the exotic exercise so often depicted by the media, thinking the unthinkable was a humdrum but fundamental activity of putting Labour back in touch with its voters.

This exercise, of course, did not escape being caught up in the shadows dancing behind Labour's intent to modernise Britain. And yet, it was a deeply conservative exercise in two important respects. First, it centred on re-establishing the primacy in public conduct of three key values. The values of work, saving and honesty were to be viewed as the great locomotive forces driving a new economic and social advance, and were intended to be the basis on which a free, prosperous and more just society could rest.

Second, it swept back to the point where debate divided amongst radical forces in Britain. In particular, the Prime Minister's lament on the division of radical impulses, between Liberal and Labour parties, was given focus: thinking the unthinkable centred on the key point of this debate which the free spirited collectivists lost almost a century ago. It was at this point that collective action and policies began to be seen as synonymous with state action with consequences that people now more readily concede. Thinking the unthinkable sought a genuine third way whereby markets would rule, but these market disciplines and entrepreneurial skills would shape new forms of collective provision.

Central to the whole exercise was a reacceptance that welfare is a most powerful agent for shaping behaviour – for good or ill – and that politicians ignore this elementary fact at enormous cost to society at large.

Welfare reform is now in retreat on each of these fronts. Welfare cuts have been pushed through Parliament against the most persistent Opposition any Government has experienced since backbench revolt brought down the Chamberlain Government in 1940. Welfare changes, masquerading as reform, have undermined the principle of work, mocked the idea of saving, and weighted public policy against people who tell the truth. The Prime Minister's intent to pick up and unite the best of those radical traditions which were riven asunder by party divisions at the turn of the century has, sadly, come to nought. In place of working through new forms of non-state collective provision, the market provision is extended and a poor law means-tested welfare is offered to an ever growing residuum. Far from all welfare reform measures adding to social inclusion, a growing number have become an ever-more powerful agent of exclusion.

The agreement on the influence welfare exerts on behaviour has been lost. Politicians spend so much of their political lives striving to reach the levers of power only to find that the levers do not, after all, release the forces of change they expected. Not so with welfare. Indeed, partly because of the declining influence of Government action in so many other areas, pulling the welfare levers still delivers a comparatively lively response. With a third of taxpayers' money now spent on welfare, most of us are well and truly connected to the other end of the welfare levers. It is therefore not without irony that politicians are again behaving in the one area where they have undoubted influence as though there was no link between what they decide and how the rest of us respond. It is the failure to hold to this aspect of the thinking the unthinkable exercise – of welfare's impact on behaviour and thereby character – that explains Labour's retreat on welfare and where the most profound long-term consequences will be felt.

Central to my concerns has been a rethinking of welfare reform as a means rather than an end in itself. The end is the kind of good society which radicals wish to see advanced. Here ideas about that society stress the importance of individuals fulfilling their potential, of balancing personal independence with a proper sense of interdependence, with the acceptance of duties which, important in themselves, also help bind citizens together. All these objectives help craft the temper of the civic culture. Viewed this way, individual measures of welfare reform are favoured not only by the degree to which they achieve their immediate objective, but also the degree to which they help further these linked characteristics of the good society. So, while helping the poor is an important objective, how the poor are helped becomes crucial. Do the means of redistribution advanced underpin or undermine the likelihood of developing fully a person's talents, and does such a strategy simultaneously help strengthen the sense of civic culture? Alternatively, are the means by which the poor are helped ones which increase their dependence while developing a 'them and us' culture?

The means by which poverty is combated is also seen as part of the wider issue of building a successful and sustainable coalition of voters. Votes now stack up differently from the pattern understood under the Attlee Government. Whether or not the age in which we live warrants the title of New Politics, it is certainly dominated by different political arithmetic. Ever since Joe Chamberlain ushered in the age of ransom, politicians have bid for the votes of one section of the community by levying taxes on another, distinct group. As the tax net spread to encompass wider circle of voters, politicians resorted to bribing voters with their own money. Such black arts could only be practised for so long.

Here is one aspect of the new political arithmetic. Voters now resist direct taxes being increased, as the increases invariably mean their own taxes going up. This view on taxes is reinforced in our aspirational society where voters inevitably identify with people above rather than below them in the social hierarchy. This is coalition voting with a vengeance and it has produced a new political terrain in which advancing the interests of the entrenched poor is made even harder.

This realignment of voter interests and attitudes has taken place over decades. The impact of a shrinking working class, and the rise of affluence, has been commented upon since the 1960s. But the pace of change has recently quickened and there is ample evidence to suggest that this will continue.

Many of the essays in this volume centre on one aspect of

the new political agenda: how to protect and promote the interests of the poor in an age when Labour can win elections without them. The moral issue of whether they should seek to do so is, sadly, distinct. Seeing that the interests of the poor were advanced was a comparatively easy exercise when the working class and the poor were practically synonymous. That is no longer the case and an important part of the new task is to establish shared interest between different groups of voters and bring the poor within that coalition. It is this building up and highlighting of common interests which underpins the reform programme I proposed as Minister for Welfare Reform and which is outlined in the first essay in this volume.

This task of building, and then maintaining a coalition of voters, will become harder. Before this voter realignment is complete, politicians wishing to be radical will have to think the unthinkable on financing additions to public services. Increases in the funding of many public services is likely to come from individuals themselves adding to that part of existing budgets which they use, rather than making that increase in expenditure through collective taxes. How this can be satisfactorily achieved will become a key constituent part of radical policies in the new millennium.

Another aspect of this new voter coalition building takes us back again to the role of how welfare can help shape behaviour. Welfare needs widespread public support if it is to prosper in the longer term. Thinking the unthinkable was about setting policy to reward good behaviour – specifically encouraging work and savings and enhancing honesty. This debate is now set to change gear. The change in emphasis will be from using welfare simply as a means to stimulate good behaviour, to providing a sanction against regularly occurring unacceptable actions. The collapse of decent behaviour in some parts of the poorest areas adds urgency to this rethink.

Increasingly, there is a demand from people living in these areas for persistently anti-social behaviour to be punished by the loss of welfare. This growing popular demand will register amongst politicians so that welfare will increasingly be made conditional on proper behaviour. The likelihood is that welfare in the 21st century will be called upon to take on the role that evangelical Christianity took in the 19th century in shaping public behaviour.

These then are some of the themes developed in the following essays. They were all delivered as talks or lectures following my resignation as Minister for Welfare Reform. The only exception is the first essay which has been written for this volume. Here, for the first time, I outline those main policies I wished to advance in Government. Some aspects of this reform agenda have been accepted. Hopefully other parts of the programme will be acted upon as the Government tries to give some semblance of welfare reform between now and the General Election. But briefings suggest that those changes likely to occur will, for example, be of the kind suggested for the industrial injuries scheme. In other words any changes are likely to be relatively modest and each one will push welfare towards a more market orientated basis. The idea of an overall reform balancing the different kinds of provision, and of how reform helps further the ideas of the good society, now look lost. Yet successful welfare reform requires an understanding of the political and social ecology of voters' lives. This vision, for the moment at least, is an idea as though it had never been.

1. The Route March to Welfare Reform

We live in a world where welfare, the Government's largest budget, significantly affects behaviour. The choice politicians have to make is to determine whether spending £100 billion of taxpayers' money supports constructive or destructive behaviour. In Opposition a commitment was made to rebalance welfare so that it would encourage work, savings, and honesty. To this end means-testing was rejected and the necessary rebalancing of the welfare budget was to come, in part, from expanding non-state forms of provision.

However, in Government, means-testing is not only being extended, but the framework for expanding non-state collective welfare has also been fudged. Here I outline the alternative programme I suggested when Minister for Welfare Reform. It involves recasting what stakeholder pensions should be, redrawing the line of responsibility between the individual and Government, sometimes pushing it in favour of the individual or firm – such as in respect of industrial injuries – or pooling it in favour of collective provision, as with unemployment insurance. The provision of compulsory stakeholder pensions offers the possibility of curtailing state welfare, but only after alternative insurance cover is built on the back of this universal, non-state provision.

Expenditure control

The first results of the general election came in late on the Thursday of polling day. From very early on it was clear that the electorate had not merely rejected the Major Government, but that they had swept it from power decisively. For a second successive occasion the first past the post system of voting had worked in Labour's favour.[1] A 10.3 per cent swing from the Conservatives resulted in a record number of Labour seats. On Saturday the new Prime Minister publicly began forming his Government. Early that morning I was offered the post of Minister for Welfare Reform.[2]

On the following Monday I met the Prime Minister and it was agreed that I would prepare a Green Paper setting out the ideas which would underpin the welfare reform programme. When the Green Paper began its drafting stage the Department was beginning its review of expenditure. It is now all too easy to forget the atmosphere in which that expenditure review was conducted.

The Government had committed itself to keeping the Tory Government's expenditure plans for the remaining two years those plans had to run. The social security bills were not only the largest part of the Government's budget, but it was widely believed that they were growing faster than any other major item of expenditure. The first public inkling of what sticking to the previous Government's expenditure plans meant came over the decision to hold to the Tory Government's proposed equalisation of benefits for single and two-parent families. I had been the only Labour Member in Opposition publicly to support these changes, so I had no difficulty with what the Government was proposing. But to make this the first announcement from a Government pledged to reform welfare ensured that cutting expenditure became the reform agenda in the eyes of all too many Labour MPs, and in the eyes of the country at large.

For a Government that prided itself on its public relations skills, such a move was little short of bizarre, particularly as the image being put over could not have been more misleading. The Government was in reality committed to a growth in welfare expenditure, as the Green Paper was to make plain. How could it be otherwise when, for example, an ever greater proportion of the population was retiring, many of them early, and most were living longer? If welfare bills did not rise, the living standards of pensioners would have to fall.

What was crucial in this debate was the message that, of this expanding welfare bill, a falling proportion would be met by taxpayers. And while welfare would be cut in some areas, those changes would come into effect only when alternative sources of welfare had been established. Preventing fraud offered the necessary quick cuts in expenditure. Here large savings could be made once the Government agreed a plan of action and then implemented it.

All these different parts of the original welfare reform scenario were presented in the Green Paper. In the meantime the Department was almost overwhelmed by the CSR, as it was called. Here the drive was focused on cutting overall expenditure. At the same time the Review was the vehicle by which each area of policy was considered. The difficulty of planning long-term reform when the pressure was on for short-term savings in public expenditure was compounded for me in that my requests to chair each of these reviews were refused.

I accepted these decisions. It was clear that the reviews were finding it difficult to pick up speed. I judged – wrongly as it turned out – that I should make the best of a near hopeless set-up while awaiting the reshuffle. I had been assured on that first Saturday morning, before accepting the Prime Minister's offer of the post of Minister for Welfare Reform, that a reshuffle would take place within six months.

I believed, again wrongly as it transpired, that to fight each of these setbacks – which as I have said, I was led to believe could only last up to six months – would serve only to foster the image that I was not a team player. That caricature of my behaviour had been spun long ago by a Labour leadership scared of fighting Trotskyite extremism. It assumed that there was a team worth playing for before the advent of Tony Blair's New Labour. Much of my efforts before Tony Blair's leadership centred on holding out hope to dispirited and often desolate Labour voters that their views and values were still voiced by Labour in Parliament.

Reaffirming old values, but presenting these values through new policies, centred around the so-called thinking the unthinkable exercise. This was another of those press phrases which all too often go under the guise of serious reporting. Thinking the unthinkable was an activity for Opposition. It never was, nor was it meant to be, a task for Government. Not one of the aspects of the thinking the unthinkable project could be remotely described as such. The whole exercise – as the first chapter details – was simply about reasserting traditional Labour values, and how these values might be realised again in an electoral terrain remarkably different from what had been traversed before.

The politics of ransom[3] had run its course. The political race for votes, by offering prizes to non-taxpayers paid for by taxpayers, was fast running out of supporters. Its appeal continues to decline as the hand of successive Chancellors digs deeper and deeper and into ever-smaller wage packets.

How could poorer people get a first-rate deal when increasingly taxpayers no longer saw their interests allied to the poor, but to those rapidly rising up the social and financial ladders? To complicate matters the issue is not a simple one of ensuring a higher income for the poor, which is clearly an important objective. Fundamental welfare reform seeks to increase the income of poorer people while at the same time extending their freedom. As Gladstone argued in one of his budget speeches, the task is to enlarge the poor's means without narrowing their freedom.[4] How to achieve these twin objectives has been the central issue I have tried to address as an MP.

Providing the poor with more money is not too hard a task, particularly at a time of rising unemployment and, consequentially, expanding Government revenue. This simple objective will be met by the Government's means-tested programme of the Working Families Tax Credit. But such an approach ghettos the poor.

Radical social policies must not simply be a matter of redistribution. Welfare reform's goal must be about advancing freedom of the poor. This objective is usually best realised within a framework of universal provision for it is within this approach that social and fiscal provision builds a floor on which the poor may safely build by their own efforts. Selective, means-tested welfare, acts as a fiscal ceiling often of such strength and durability that the poor are unable to push themselves through by the sheer dint of their own effort.

One objective of thinking the unthinkable was to show that it was to society's advantage as a whole to seek new ways – including partnerships with the private sector – of extending universalism. This involved painting a view of how societies function, and particularly how best to maximise the natural forces within them for social and economic progress. Central to this exercise has been the stress I have put on striking the right balance between altruism and self-interest.[5] And here one aspect of this exercise has been to emphasise the role of character, which develops in part through the way individuals respond to the prevailing public culture, as well as the incentives and penalties inevitably involved in Government fiscal and social policies.

This rethinking exercise failed to carry important sections of Labour backbenchers. In Opposition these ideas gained currency partly because the leadership let it be known that it was along these lines that it would shape policy once in Government. But many Labour MPs viewed the language I used as coming straight from the Tory glossary. The truth is that the framework to which I worked, and the language I used, could not have been a more traditional Labour one, but fashioned before the advent of state monopoly welfare. Caught, as many Labour MPs were, like Lot's wife, frozen in a backward looking glance to the legislative programme of the post-war Labour Governments, the opportunity to enact a new agenda which advanced traditional Labour values was lost. Ideas on establishing a pro-active welfare, set out in *Making Welfare Work*[6], for example, are being implemented, thanks to the drive of the Chancellor. But the full programme I wish to see implemented waits for another Government in another Parliament. Here I set out a summary of that programme.

It was not until the final three months of my time as Minister that the Prime Minister directed the DSS that I should spearhead an anti-fraud strategy and that I should submit my aims directly to him on where to take the year-long debate on stakeholder pensions.

Signposts to reform

Every time the Green Paper was discussed the chances were that someone would talk in terms of a new Beveridge. That is how the Prime Minister referred to it in his draft introduction for the text. But, to be honest, the exercise this time was of a different nature. The form of state welfare begun by Lloyd George had been largely completed by Beveridge.

Beveridge's objective was to universalise state welfare, and his record as a reformer is unparalleled. But the debate no longer centres on extending this form of provision. Indeed, in some important instances state welfare is part of the problem. Welfare reform is now a radically different undertaking.

It entails, first, standing back and registering which forms of welfare are undermining the verities upon which prosperous and free societies are built. It is also necessary to be clear about the values and objectives which welfare should promote. Only then is it possible to develop specific welfare reform policies.

There was never any question that welfare reform would come in the form of a one-off, big bang project. No politician who had witnessed, for example, how a single reform like the Child Support Agency had so quickly descended into chaos could sensibly advocate throwing the entire welfare jigsaw puzzle into the air in a single act. Rather, the process of welfare reform was seen as a route march along which there would be a series of mini bangs – or reforms. And, to ensure the success of this march, it was necessary at the outset to provide a map and compass for this journey. The map had ten signposts. These were to:

- Ensure that people who can work do work.
- Encourage honesty.
- Promote greater self provision.
- Root out fraud.
- Remove barriers to claiming benefit.
- Promote social cohesion.
- Support families.
- Help individuals to grow to their full potential.
- Strengthen civil society.
- Maximise public confidence in the welfare institutions.

The reform programme – countering fraud
Countering fraud was not the first or even the only item on the reform agenda. It was, however, one for which a programme was published before I resigned as Minister.

Three months or so before that event occurred one of the Prime Minister's private secretaries came to my office. He reported that, now the Green Paper had been published, the

Prime Minister wished me to take responsibility for designing the Government's counter-fraud strategy. This had been the responsibility of another Minister in the department since the election. The aim had been to produce a Green Paper, but no draft Green Paper was in sight.

To advance this objective I was given one of the DSS's most talented civil servants, Robert Devereux, and the most talented outsider, Jim Gee. The latter had been the person who had mastered the means by which fraudulent social security claims are made and how best to counter them. The specialist adviser to the Social Security Select Committee in the previous Parliament was given a contract with the Department to work specifically on the countering fraud brief. A small team of outside experts was also assembled to help shape and comment on the draft Green Paper. In addition a panel of counter-fraud experts working in some of this country's most important firms and institutions was assembled to comment in detail once a draft Green Paper was completed. Within 12 weeks the Green Paper was published.

A lack of vision
And the Green Paper is there for the reading. It has since been followed by a White Paper, the aim of which was to firm up its proposals. Yet the White Paper sets out principles for tackling fraud which are themselves vaguer than the principles set out in the Green Paper. Developing an anti-fraud culture, designing policies and systems to minimise fraud, creating an anti-fraud environment and developing an anti-fraud profession – the main agenda discussed in the Green Paper – have been replaced by 'getting it right',

'keeping it right', 'putting it right', and 'making sure our strategy works'. The two documents could profitably have been published in reverse order.

Equally important is the Government's apparent failure to appreciate the extent to which an effective counter-fraud strategy must be as imaginative and proactive as, unfortunately, the fraudsters themselves. It requires running merely to stay in the same place. It must also seriously base much of the strategy on devolving power to local staff – where most of the knowledge required is to be found.

Within months of the General Election I put forward the idea of a pilot project in one or two benefit offices so that each office would control its total budget. At present the politician is obsessed with hacking back on the 3 per cent of the total budget which covers staff costs. The remaining 97 per cent of the budget is what is euphemistically called demand-led. The Exeter DSS office made the case that, should they be given a three-year budget, they would deliver within that time a saving in benefit payments which would be agreed in advance with the DSS. They would spend more in the first year of this total budget in staff costs to secure the system, which would pay real dividends in subsequent years. Giving a local office control of its total budget would allow the local management and staff – the only ones who know what is actually going on at a grassroots level – to prevent much fraud entering into the system. No action has been taken on this and a whole range of reforms I proposed while Minister. The Government's progress on tackling fraud, against the objectives set out in the Green Paper, is there for anyone who wishes to judge.

Pensions guide

The current system of pensions throws up a complicated pattern of provision and coverage. Practically everyone qualifies for what is called the State Retirement Pension. They do so either on the contributions which they have made themselves during their working life, or through the contributions their husbands have made. From 1965 the basic State Retirement Pension has been paid at a lower level than the standard means-tested pension which guarantees a minimum level of income for those pensioners without adequate additional pensions or savings.

When this Government came to office the means-tested pension was known as Income Support. It has now been renamed as a Minimum Income Guarantee (MIG) for pensioners and is paid at a more generous level. Unlike the State Retirement Pension, which is increased in line with prices, the MIG is uprated in line with earnings.

Running alongside this provision, and often pre-dating it, have been the pensions paid by companies to former employees. Half the working population are in occupational pension schemes and as each year goes by a greater proportion of pensioners gain a work's pension.

In order to ensure that all other workers who are not in an occupational scheme are not dependent simply on the State Retirement Pension – and thereby on means-tested support – the last Labour Government introduced in 1978 a wage related pension called the State Earnings

Related Pension (SERPS). The incoming Conservative Government in 1979 debated whether or not it should abolish serps. It decided on balance not to do so. It made major cuts in 1986 and 1995 in the value of what future SERPS pensioners may gain from the scheme. As an alternative attraction to SERPS the Conservative Government introduced what are known as personal pensions. Subsidies from the National Insurance Fund are paid to individuals who opt out of serps for either a personal or occupational pension.

Personal pensions have had a troubled history. Around 2.5 million workers opted out of occupational schemes into personal pensions, or joined a personal scheme when they were eligible for occupational pension membership. Practically all these individuals are now building up a lower pension entitlement than they would otherwise have gained if they had stayed in their occupational scheme. Membership of such schemes brings with them generous contributions from employers. There have been 5.4 million sales of personal pensions.

The present Government intends to abolish SERPS for new members from April 2002 (at the earliest). It is introducing two new kinds of pensions. People with annual earnings below £9,500 will be encouraged to become members of what will be called the State Second Pension.

Those earnings above this level, and in no other second pension scheme, will be encouraged by means of rebates, to take out what will be called a new Stakeholder Pension. The salient features of Stakeholder pensions are that they will be funded and will be aimed at those earning between £9,500 and £20,000.

While one aim of the Government's reforms is to simplify pensions, if all these reforms come to fruition, pension provision will include:

- the State Retirement Pension
- the Minimum Income Guarantee for pensioners
- SERPS
- occupational pensions
- personal pensions
- State Second Pensions
- Stakeholder pensions

Stakeholder pension

At the same time as I was invited to take responsibility for the counter-fraud Green Paper I was also told that the Prime Minister would welcome my views on the Stakeholder Pension. Within a couple of days I had drafted the outlines of a stakeholder pension scheme.

The challenge the Government faces on pensions can be stated clearly. Millions of pensioners are poor, and many millions more exist on the margins of poverty. The gap between the richest and the poorest pensioners is set to grow. Cuts in the State Earnings Related Pension Scheme (SERPs) entitlement, together with the falling relative value of the State pension, will, within a few decades, result in a standard of living for those pensioners without company or private pension lower in relative terms than many pensioners gained in the late 1970s. This outcome is most clearly evident in the most recent quinquennium review published by the Government Actuary.[7] The Government's own Pension Provision Group expects that the poorest pensioners will have to rely on income support to an *increasing extent* unless successful reforms are put in place.[8]

The Government has responded to this challenge in two ways. It has introduced what it calls a Minimum Income Guarantee (MIG) to help today's poor pensioners and those who will be retiring into poverty in the not too distant future. While possessing a rather posh name the MIG is but the latest in a long line of means-tested benefits.

Pensioners can claim the guarantee only if their income is below a set level. This eligibility level, however, is raised in line with earnings. The national insurance retirement pension – for which people have had to pay contributions, unlike the MIG – is reviewed in line with prices only. As earnings overall advance more rapidly than prices, the difference in value between these two pension levels is growing. As this gap widens so the sum needed to be saved to ensure an income above the MIG level grows. And, as more and more people in work on low wages realise the futility of saving when every penny so saved is taken from the MIG which is gained by people with little or no savings, fewer and fewer people on low income will save.

To compound this error comes the second action of the Government – the introduction of Stakeholder Pensions. The contributions to this pension are voluntary. Stakeholder pensions are to be aimed at workers earning between

£9,500 and £20,000 annually. But this group will have to save a great deal, and be lucky in picking an institution which is exceptional in its investment record, to be financially better off than by simply relying on an income from MIG. The results are not difficult to predict. The focus groups,[9] who were made up of the very people for whom stakeholder has been designed, report few of this target group will be buying stakeholder pensions.[10]

The Government needs to go back and consider the four objectives it set itself in respect of pensions. These are to reduce social exclusion; to gain a reduction in the role of state welfare; progressively to disengage from means tests; and to ensure a major switch towards funded pension provision. A universal compulsory funded stakeholder pension scheme is a prerequisite for success on each of these four fronts.

To achieve each of these four objectives the stakeholder reform I advocated in Government had to break with conventional wisdom in two important respects. The first break centred on the level at which the stakeholder pension should be paid. The best occupational schemes aim for nearly two-thirds of working income in retirement.[11] This is not a realistic goal for a stakeholder scheme. The primary purpose of such a scheme must be to offer a guaranteed minimum pension income which is generous enough for a stakeholder pensioner to be above means-tested assistance eligibility.[12] A two-thirds income on retirement is a desirable aim which should be sought by way of additional voluntary pension provision on top of the stakeholder base.

Deciding the best way to deliver this minimum but adequate pension resulted in a second break with traditional thinking. The form of stakeholder pension I advocated in Government offered a guarantee set at a point of average earnings which would ensure that pensioners were free from means-tested assistance. This guarantee would be delivered by payments from the national insurance scheme – which pays the existing state retirement pension – together with a growing part coming from funded sources. The scheme was not designed to provide separate pots of capital from which individuals would draw a pension entitlement, as do personal pension schemes. Once a guarantee is given, ensuring that every pensioner will have an income above means-tested welfare, there is no need to force pensioners into buying an annuity.[13]

While this pension guarantee is a flat-rate payment, it cannot be bought on the open market. Any such guarantee has to be backed by the whole community which provides the surety for it. Such a guarantee is an attractive proposition not only to lower paid workers, for whom stakeholder may provide their only source of retirement income, but also to people on higher earnings. It is the attractiveness of this guarantee, which cannot be bought elsewhere, that offers the political basis for winning approval for graduated contributions to the scheme. These graduated dues provide the funds to pay the contributions each year of the working poor, and those outside the labour market, such as carers, whose role in society is to be part rewarded by full membership of the stakeholder scheme.

Following the mis-selling scandal there is widespread unease about private insurance companies. I do not believe the Government can compel individuals to save through such companies. The funded side of the scheme would therefore be sold through Approved Welfare Suppliers (AWSs). The new suppliers could be established by a single employer, or a group of employers, a single trade union, or a group of trade unions, or by other groups. Present pension providers would seek Approved Welfare Supplier status. Such an approach would allow stakeholder pensions to be provided as the first tranche of any occupational pension plan. The only stipulation would be that all AWSs – including that part of any occupational scheme – would have to be membership-owned organisations. Such organisations would be carefully regulated. The AWS representatives, together with public trustees, would set the investment policy for all stakeholder pension schemes.

The introduction of a compulsory stakeholder pension scheme would prevent scheme members inheriting poverty in old age. The stakeholder pension scheme would come into play on a set vesting day. A core requirement of the scheme was that, on a vesting day, all 21-year olds in work – or whatever starting age was decided upon – would be required to take out a stakeholder pension. Each year each new group of 21-year old workers would be required to become members of a stakeholder pension scheme. It would also be possible, however, to modify the scheme without destroying its intrinsic value by allowing older workers to join and gain partial benefits from their contributions.

Either way the scheme was not designed to alleviate the poverty and hardship experienced by many of today's pensioners. Other measures are necessary to tackle this urgent but distinct issue. And these measures should be designed to support and not undermine the longer-term stakeholder reform. As Alison Dash and Steve Webb have shown, the older pensioners are, generally speaking, the poorer they are.[14] Following their lead, the suggestion is for a major increase in the national insurance retirement pension, kicking in after 15 years of retirement.

Such a reform is also an attractive proposition for those already on a reasonable pension. This group is only too aware how they need to eat into their savings during each year of retirement. A significant increase in the national insurance pension at 80 is therefore an income addition which will be welcomed by somewhat better-off pensioners. A reform strategy along these lines therefore widens considerably the constituency supporting it.

The reform is also attractive to the wider electorate in that it does nothing to lessen anybody's impulse to save for retirement; the addition is not effective until 15 years after the state retirement pension becomes payable for men and 20 years for women. No rational person is going to stop saving on this score. More importantly, because the national insurance pension is not means-tested, it is known that all savings will be kept in addition to whatever the stakeholder pension is at 65 (if that is the age set for retirement), and the enhanced value of the state retirement pension component of stakeholder at the age of 80.

Stakeholder pensions open up other reforms: life cover and long-term care

Making stakeholder pensions universal along the lines suggested here opens up a different approach to the reform of other parts of the welfare state than that now being adopted by the Government. Two of the assumptions made in Opposition about welfare were, first, that as national income rose, so too would welfare expenditure. And, second, that alternative forms of provision would be in place before state provision was curtailed or withdrawn.

This is not the approach the Government has adopted, although hopefully it will become so. In Opposition Labour accused the Thatcher and Major Governments of hacking at the foundations of the national insurance scheme and of pushing on to means-tested assistance millions of people who had a legitimate expectation to draw insurance benefits. That same approach is, however, continued in the Welfare Reform and Pensions Act.

Introducing Stakeholder pensions along the lines outlined here would have allowed two further reforms to fit easily into place. A universal stakeholder scheme would allow life insurance to be cheaply and comprehensively built on the back of the pension scheme. With universal provision, risks are pooled in the biggest pool possible, and average insurance costs cut to a minimum. The prevention of cherry-picking also means that taxpayers are not presented with the bills for those people whom insurance companies do not wish to cover.

A universal stakeholder pension scheme would therefore allow the closure of the existing national insurance widow's benefit, and soon to be widower's benefit. Each age cohort coming into the stakeholder scheme would have life cover included in their pension scheme membership. The breadth of cover this achieved would allow the closure of the current national insurance bereavement coverage scheme to new entrants to the labour market, and to older workers too if they were brought into the pension scheme as partial beneficiaries.

A stakeholder pension scheme along these lines could also offer the basis for long-term care insurance similar to the model advocated for the reform of bereavement benefit. Each cohort coming into stakeholder provision could be provided with long-term care insurance. Because this insurance scheme would be compulsory, with all of the age group becoming members, the costs of insurance would again be kept to a minimum.

Alternatively, long-term care insurance could be extended to all those currently in work, as well as to pensioners. How such a scheme could work, and the basis on which it would be built, has been described in *How to Pay for the Future*.[15] Contributions would be collected from that much larger group and the scheme would also run on a pay-as-you-go basis.

Rebalancing risk and responsibilities

Part of the immediate post-war political settlement was for the Government to underwrite risks which had previously been met by individuals and their families. Reviewing who, Government or individual, should meet which risks in the future was to be part of the reform agenda. And the direction of change would not automatically be one way, i.e. from state to individual. The cost of industrial injuries would be returned from taxpayers to employers. A greater proportion of the risk associated with starting a job, on the other hand, would be met by taxpayers. Abolishing housing benefit, thereby giving tenants the responsibility to meet their rent directly, would significantly increase the freedom of many people in the rented sector.

Industrial injuries

A separate industrial injuries fund, established in the early post-war period, was transferred to the National Insurance Fund in 1973. No charge is levied on those employers responsible for the injury, maiming or death of employees. The cost of benefits paid to these employees is met fully by taxpayers, costing them around £750 million a year.

The proposal I made as Minister was that the cost of industrial injuries should be transferred to employers. A three-stage reform was envisaged. The first move was to separate the administration of the Industrial Injuries Scheme from the National Insurance Fund. Employer organisations would be required to run this part of the fund. Next, a set timetable would be established in which employers would assume a greater share of the cost of the scheme. Third, employers would be free to change the form of the fund. They may decide, for example, to franchise out to an insurance company their responsibility for the scheme. But, if practice in other countries is any guide, it is likely that employer mutuals would be established.

Such a reform would transfer the cost of industrial injuries from taxpayers to those responsible for the cost; would lead to the development of a system of premiums related to the risks incurred by individuals working in particular firms; might lead to a possible fall in industrial injuries; could open the possibility of charging employers the NHS costs resulting from industrial injuries and, finally, a reform such as this could help develop new institutions of civil society.

Unemployment insurance
Welfare was not to be reformed by applying inflexible dogma to each and every part of the budget. Crudely shifting much of the bill currently met by taxpayers on to individuals and households was never part of the scheme I envisaged. Reforming industrial injury, so that employers resumed costs previously borne by Government, is, I believe, the right direction. A totally different approach is required for reforming insurance against unemployment. Here the balance is for the community to take a more proactive role, as well as to underwrite to a greater extent the costs of the greater risks of moving back into and being able to stay in work. A reform reflecting this awareness, however, would change the welfare culture, adding to a growing emphasis on Government being responsible for helping people back into work.

Benefits paid to the unemployed need to reflect the growing flexibility, as it is called, in the labour market. Recent research from the Rowntree Foundation shows that three-quarters of women moving from benefit into work take a flexible job, as do two-thirds of men.[16] 29 per cent of women and 39 per cent of men take a 'downgraded' job in order to get back to work, while 16 and 20 per cent respectively take temporary work.

Benefits paid to the unemployed need to reflect this growing flexibility or uncertainty in the labour market. In an age of full employment, benefit was paid for 12 months. In an age of high unemployment – there are still 1.15 million registered unemployed last year compared to around 250,000 in 1955, the Jobseeker's allowance insurance benefit is paid for only six months. Once this right is exhausted claimants may be eligible for means-tested JSA where the income of partners is taken into account. Many of these partners then cease working. Once people have used up their entitlement to six months' JSA insurance benefit, they become eligible again only after two years' contributions.

The reform proposed that the rules for requalifying – which are currently complicated and difficult to understand – should be weighted to compensate risks now all too often associated with returning to work. The suggestion was to set requalifying conditions at 13 consecutive contributions (13 weeks in work is taken now by the New Deal as sustained employment). Once these contributions have been paid benefit would be extended for a further 13 weeks. The new eligibility rules would, of course, be policed by the extension of the New Deal where claimants thought to be abusing benefit would be quickly offered a full-time option instead of benefit. The aim would be to test how such a change affected claimants' behaviour. The qualifying rules would, if necessary, be adjusted.

The results of such a reform would weight the risk of returning to work in an uncertain labour market in favour of claimants. Many new jobs turn out to be temporary, but not all. It is impossible to say which might result in permanent employment. A fast-track route to requalifying rebalances the rewards in favour of the risk-takers.

Such a reform would also have an important impact on the motivation of the partners of the unemployed. At present it pays those partners in modest or low-paid employment not to work once unemployment strikes a household and the claimant is on means-tested JSA. The earnings of a partner do not affect the payment of insurance benefit.

Housing costs
Housing benefit expenditure currently stands at £11.5 billion, a sum which has been growing at 11 per cent in real terms over the last six years. Expenditure is growing fastest for claimants in housing association or private tenancies – a 20 per cent rise in real terms during the 1990s compared to a 6 per cent rise for the benefit paid to council tenants. Housing benefit has been growing faster than the average growth in the welfare bill largely due to the increase in the average value of the benefit paid. And the average value of the benefit paid has been rising largely because of the rise in rents.

The latest leaks from the Government indicate that it has abandoned radical reform of housing benefit. Radical reform is too expensive, or so the spin goes. But not to reform housing benefit is also expensive. The projected increase in the housing benefit budget over the life of this Parliament was put at £3 billion when I was minister and part of a joint DETR and DSS working party. The proposal I made was to bring forward that sum into the current benefit account. This additional money would be used to buy out claimants of housing benefit.

The £3 billion sum would allow housing benefit payments to be increased by around 25 per cent. Housing benefit would therefore cease to exist. Existing claimants would have a weekly income which would include the sum which was paid as housing benefit, plus the 25 per cent increase, and they would pay their rent from their total weekly income. New eligible applicants would have an average rent payment for their area and type of accommodation paid as part of their weekly benefit. Tenants would therefore have an interest in resisting rent increases, or in bargaining over new tenancies, as do tenants who currently pay the whole of their rent from their earned income.

The disadvantages of this approach to reform are that it will cost £3 billion. Yet this is a sum which will be paid anyway if reform is not attempted. The advantages of the approach I made are that it marks the end of housing benefit; reimposes on tenants for the first time since housing benefit came into existence, the obligation of meeting their rent[17] just as they do with food, heating, lighting and anything else in their budgets; and signals the start of a much wider market in the rented sector.

Such a reform would mark a major change in the housing market which would be brought about largely by the freedom tenants would have to shop around if they so wished. It is, however, impossible to gain the first advantage – a more market-orientated approach – without conceding tenants that freedom. Under the current system tenants on housing benefit do not gain if they move to cheaper accommodation. All that changes is the size of their housing benefit, which is often paid directly to the landlords. Under the proposed reform, tenants wishing to move to cheaper accommodation would pocket the whole of the difference between their new rents and those they used to pay. The disposable income of the tenant rises, tenant mobility is increased, and tenant turnover is enlarged.

Flexible and proactive
Fifty years ago, the vast majority of claimants for social security were pensioners. Now most are of working age. Then, the major aim of welfare was to ensure the prompt payment of supplementary pensions to the poorest pensioners. Now, welfare has the duty of helping people back into work while seeing that their benefits are delivered promptly and accurately.

Many single mothers successfully continue being the main parent for their children while meeting all the demands of a job. Even so, the largest group of working age claimants is single mothers. Single parents – for one in ten are fathers – have a right to remain on benefit until their youngest child is 16.

The Government has made a welcome step in establishing a proactive welfare state for single parents, but the approach has some not so hidden assumptions which leave the programme stranded without much public support and largely ignored by most single parents. The Government's spin in its earlier days was that single mothers should work, with the age of their children being left deliberately vague. That single parents should work was an implicit threat, although, when challenged directly on this, the Government quickly retreated, assuring everyone that the programme was voluntary.

The public, unsurprisingly, registered its unease at the

Government's approach. While they are unaware of the figures – why should they be otherwise as the Government does not publicise them – their gut reaction is one of wanting to help single parents do the best for their children, knowing that most of the single mothers get back to work just as soon as opportunities arise, and when they believe it right to combine this task with that of looking after their family. The public also know that there is a hard core of mothers intent on staying on welfare, whatever their family circumstances.

These decent natural instincts of the majority of single parents need to be encouraged by moving more quickly to proactive welfare. The aim of the reform was to replace a benefit service where the only question to the claimant was 'where is the father of your child?', with no more questions being asked for up to 20 or more years. Regular meetings on training and career prospects should become an automatic part of the benefit service, not a voluntary option, as it is now. The objective was to develop a service which, while meeting the income needs of single parents, would give attention to what training skills could be acquired while they are on benefit; what child care facilities were available; and what benefit would still be paid when the claimant moved into part or full-time work. 'This is the first day of the rest of your life. How do you wish to make the most of it?' must be the theme around which Income Support develops for single mothers, and for other claimants below retirement age. This was the commitment in Opposition.

Most families cannot earn fully when their children are very young. While some mothers begin work while their children are very young, the beginning of schooling coincides with many more mothers entering at least part-time work. Once children are in secondary schools still more mothers enter work, often full-time.

This work pattern, of increasing labour market participation as children get older, should be matched by a more flexible pattern of benefits. And it is at this point that pressure should be rightly applied to that core of single parents who have no intention of working and who will stay on welfare as long as they possibly can. It is during the very earliest years of childhood that a family budget – be they one or two parent – is under greatest strain. Child benefit should therefore be weighted to children under five. Likewise, the right to income support up to the sixteenth birthday of the youngest child should be moved down, step by step, towards the eleventh birthday of the youngest child as a point up to which benefit is automatically paid to single parents. Benefit would not be paid unconditionally. Single mothers would be required to attend interviews regularly and plan how they wish to develop their skills for return at some point to the labour market.

The Child Support Act

The number of single mothers on benefit who benefited from maintenance payments collapsed during the 1980s –from around 65 per cent in 1975 to 14 per cent in 1994[18]. The cost to taxpayers of the failure of fathers to support their children amounts to almost 4p in the standard rate of tax. The CSA aimed at reversing this trend, enforcing the financial responsibilities of parents after they ceased to live together, and equally importantly, leading to 'absent' parents maintaining contact with their children. Despite spending £800m in running the new service, the numbers paying maintenance has risen by only four percentage points. Large numbers of fathers refused to pay anything, little extra money is raised in maintenance and few users or politicians understand how maintenance liability was computed.

I proposed a three part reform. First, the calculations had to be made simple.[19] The CSA regulations remain so complicated that no single member of staff can be trained to answer all enquiries. 95 per cent of staff time is currently committed to calculating maintenance awards leaving only 5 per cent for their enforcement. The aim of reform was to reverse the proportions of time spent on such tasks. A simple CSA tax could be imposed. This part of the reform has thankfully been accepted although, amazingly, the first discussions in the Department would have led to an even more complicated and unintelligible formula.

Second, the body collecting CSA payments must change. At present it is carried out by a DSS agency – a body geared to paying out money, not collecting it. The Inland Revenue is the body charged with collecting revenue for the Government. It is obviously the body which should be charged with this role for maintenance payments.

Third, the single tax formula has to be set at a lower level than is proposed by the Government.[20] The Government is proposing a tax rate of 15, 20 or 25 per cent for a one, two and third child maintenance assessment. I believe the rates should be at the most 10, 15 and 20 per cent. There is a trade off in the level of maintenance payments and greater compliance. The aim must be to persuade more fathers, usually, to pay maintenance regularly.

The current formula is Treasury driven, i.e., its aim is to raise roughly the same sums as does the existing regime. One reason why I raised the issue of the collapse in maintenance payments for claimants on benefits, when almost no one else thought it an issue, was the bill which taxpayers were forced to pick up. I also thought it important too for children to know that both parents played important roles in their upbringing. So I in no way omit taxpayers from this discussion as all too many politicians still do. But I now believe that another objective has to take precedence in order that the legitimate demands of taxpayers can effectively be met in the longer term.

My belief is that if the reform is not successful this time, the whole CSA machinery will collapse. This is a risk which is real and which must be guarded against. A lower tax take for maintenance than is being proposed by the Government will increase public pressure on non-payers to comply. The mobilising of the 'absent' father's peer group pressure is totally ignored by the Government. 'You are being asked to pay 10p tax maintenance. But I pay an extra 5p on each pound earned. Why don't you pay?' has to become part of the common culture. A higher maintenance tax can be brought in at a later date for all new claims once the reforms are seen to be working. In addition, the Revenue must be given the responsibility for collection.

Final destination

To what kind of new country would this route march lead? It would be one in which there was a recognition that, no matter how powerful the state, most advances come from individual action and from individual motivation. There would be a clear appreciation of human nature and the extent to which self interest drives individuals. As there will be a full acceptance of the extent to which welfare affects motives and behaviour, there would therefore be a growing disengagement from means-tested provision and an acceptance that the right to other benefits will be conditional.

It would be a country with more not less welfare. There would be an increase in collective welfare provision but a far smaller proportion being provided by the State. State provided welfare would represent a declining proportion of the total bill. The State will become recognisably one amongst a number of major welfare providers. More of the collective welfare would be provided through member-owned organisations which themselves become a major part of a new constitutional settlement.

Such a vision is still tantalisingly within our reach.

Footnotes
1 The 1992 election gave the Conservatives an amazing 7.5 per cent lead over Labour in the popular vote but a mere 21 seat majority in the House of Commons.
2 It appears that my wish to think about the post for some time led to the Prime Minister postponing the appointment of the majority of his Cabinet, or at least the announcements of those posts were not made until I had accepted the post of Minister for Welfare Reform.
3 'The Doctrine of Ransom – Mark II', in *Reflections on*

Welfare Reform, SMF, 1998.
4 Cited in Pat Thane, 'Government and Society in England and Wales, 1750–1914', in *Cambridge Social History of Britain*, Vol 3, ed F M L Thompson, CUP, 1996, 27.
5 *Altruism, Self-Interest and the Sustainability of Welfare*, Sarum College, Salisbury, 29 September 1999.
6 *Making Welfare Work*, ICS, 1995
7 GAD Report, *National Insurance Estimates*, Cm 4406, 1999, p. 14
8 *We all need pensions – the prospects for pension provision*, Report of the Pension Provision Group, HMSO, 1998, 52.
9 *Consumer Research into Stakeholder Pensions*, conducted by Frank Research on behalf of Pearl Assurance, July/August, 1999.
10 NatWest, Pensions Index, Vol IV, Winter 1999, 4
11 Though, admittedly, few workers retire with full benefits. Less than one per cent, in fact.
12 The Government has to its credit designed the State Second Pension catering for workers earning up to £9,500 a year as a flat-rate scheme. But how long will these workers claiming this benefit in full remain above means-tested support?
13 A major aim of annuities is to ensure that pensioners spread their income which has been gained with the help of tax concessions over retirement in a way which is most likely to make them independent of means-tested support. A guarantee above means-tested support ensures this goal is achieved. How pensioners manage

their affairs then is their business, and not the Government.
14 Alison Dash and Steve Webb, *A New Future for State Pensions*, Centre for Reform, 1999.
15 *How To Pay For The Future: Building a Stakeholder's Welfare*, Institute of Community Studies, 1996.
16 JRF Briefing: *Social Protection and Welfare Beyond Work*, nd, 3. Some commentators argue, rightly, that some of these workers, and maybe many of them, look for flexible jobs. The issue, however, is whether the benefit system supports such a choice or hinders it.
17 An obligation many tenants would welcome.
18 Has the number claiming maintenance?
19 This was the weight of the evidence from the CAB and Welfare Rights Organisations when giving evidence to the Select Committee in the last parliament.
20 Taxpayers would need to guarantee to the parent with care any difference between the current maintenance payment and the new sum. However, as income rises, maintenance tax would similarly rise so the guarantee would be a short-term one.

2. What Then Was Unthinkable?*

There has understandably been much speculation and fun over the phrase 'thinking the unthinkable'. I am sorry to disappoint, but it was not a command uttered to me by the Prime Minister when he appointed me as Welfare Reform Minister. My main interest has always been to help develop policies that could work and, at the same time, advance a fairer society. If a catchphrase is needed then 'thinking the workable' is, I hope, a more accurate description of what I have been about these past three decades or more.

And yet thinking the unthinkable had a central place in welfare reform. But even here the media continue, engagingly, to miss the timing of the whole project. My stress on the past tense will have hopefully made the point.

Thinking the unthinkable was never meant to be a task for Government. It was, however, a central activity in Opposition. Helping the party confront what had become, for it, unthinkable was also everything to do with proposing workable policies. Where thinking the unthinkable took policy was to be the cornerstone on which the welfare reform programme would build once the electorate had signalled the go ahead. Indeed, one reason why the electorate was prepared to give Labour the keys of office was because thinking the unthinkable on welfare had been undertaken prior to May 1997 and, more importantly, that such thinking was believed to have been accepted by the leadership.

There were five important areas where thinking the unthinkable was urgent for Old Labour. The first was with regard to the size and growth of the social security budget, although the question of the size of that budget was and is not quite as straightforward as it is sometimes made to sound. Much of welfare's expansion has understandably won widespread public support. There is, however, one area which now looks out of control. It is here, on the means-tested budget, that attention should be directed, both because of the rate of growth of expenditure, and the effect that this use of taxpayers' money has on the behaviour of recipients.

The second area of challenge was to the belief that welfare was an island unto itself. Far from being so, welfare is inextricably bound up with the everyday process of life. What happens in welfare has an immediate impact not merely on a person's income, but also on how they shape their longer-term response to that welfare expenditure.

The third area of revisionism took place in challenging the idea that welfare should be based on the idea of citizenship rather than on earned contributions to society. Thinking the unthinkable here challenged the idea that the main impulse for welfare sprang from altruism and that this alone was a principle both robust enough, and with such widespread popular support, that it could be the basis on which welfare's distribution was decided.

The fourth area where thinking the unthinkable occurred was on the question of universal benefits. Thinking the unthinkable maintained that universalism, and the delivery of such benefits, could be viewed as two distinct issues. Universal provision could and should be achieved sometimes through partnership with the private and mutual sectors. Indeed, in some instances, it is only through such partnership that universal provision may be achieved.

The fifth and last issue on thinking the unthinkable's agenda centred around a renaissance of civil society. Although the term civil society was not then in common currency, the plans for building up membership-owned organisations, separate from Government on the one hand and from privately owned companies on the other, was intrinsic to the thinking the unthinkable process. Owning the new welfare state was the quid pro quo of setting aside more of today's income to meet tomorrow's welfare demands.

Why welfare is the big issue

On a number of occasions the Prime Minister has said that reforming welfare is the big issue facing the Government. Many commentators believe that welfare holds the political centre stage simply because of the growth of its budget during the post-war period. Yet, as I hope to argue, this is only part of a whole range of reasons why welfare has moved to the centre of the political debate.

Welfare expenditure has certainly grown disproportionately in comparison with the rise in national income. Growing at twice the rate of the economy, social security payments now account for 13 per cent of GDP – up from 5 per cent less than four decades ago.[1] But it is not simply a matter of the size of the budget, or simply its growth, although these are not issues which should be dismissed. It is, rather, on the causes and consequences of such growth that most attention should be focused. Moreover, it was in explaining why so much of welfare expenditure had eroded life's decencies that much thinking of the unthinkable took place.

Causes of welfare expenditure

There are a number of reasons which account for welfare expenditure's eightfold increase in real terms since 1948. The first reason is the very obvious one. More people are now eligible for the very same structure of benefits that came into operation over 50 years ago. There are now, for example, almost three times the number of people eligible for the retirement pension.

The second reason that helps to account for this eightfold increase in real terms in welfare expenditure is again straightforward. As national income has risen so too has the real value of welfare benefits – by two and a half times.

A third factor accounting for the increase in the welfare bill comes from a raft of new benefits introduced mainly for people with disabilities. The Attendance Allowance and Mobility Allowance were the precursors of a whole range of new benefits for people with disabilities. At the same time eligibility for other benefits has been extended.

It is however on the fourth reason underlying the growth of the welfare bill that I intend to concentrate. Welfare expenditure has not been rising uniformly across all benefits. It is where it has grown fastest that the greatest concern lies and for reasons that go far beyond the mere cost.

Welfare can be classified under three main headings. There are first of all those benefits operating under national insurance principles. Strict contribution conditions have to be fulfilled before benefits are paid. Examples of such benefits are the retirement pension, and the contributory jobseekers' allowance.

A second category of benefits is those known as non-contributory insurance benefits. People qualify for help by being deemed to be in a particular category of need, eg a disability, and the benefits are paid irrespective of the income of the recipient. Examples here are the benefits which help to offset the costs of disability and which were initiated with the introduction in the 1970s of the mobility allowance attendance allowance and the invalid care allowance.

A third category of welfare is offered only after a test of income and capital. While the post-war welfare settlement was to be built around the insurance principle it was always envisaged that there would be a means-tested element in the post-war welfare state. But the means-test role was planned to be residual to the comprehensive coverage offered by a fully-fledged national insurance scheme. For it to be otherwise risked undermining the appeal and attraction of the insurance scheme.

Matters turned out rather differently. The safety net national assistance scheme, which has been renamed on numerous occasions and currently sails under the colours of income support, is now one of the major welfare players. Means-tested help is also now offered in addition to income support in the form of supplements to low wages, help with the cost of housing and meeting council tax bills, meeting the cost of optical and dental care, covering the cost of school dinners and so on.

In 1948, when the modern welfare state came into existence, for every one pound spent on means-tested help, over £4 went in the payment of insurance benefits. In 1992, for the first time since establishing a modern welfare state, less than half of the social security budget went in financing insurance benefits. This is a transformation in the ordering of the welfare state as dramatic as it is significant for the welfare of the wider society.

While the growth of means-tested welfare was apparent throughout the post-war period, its relative importance was dramatically changed in the years following the election of the first Thatcher Government. It is important for us to pause and consider briefly how relative welfare expenditure has changed during this period, for it is around questioning the growing dominance of means-testing that part of thinking the unthinkable took place.

The figures in the table illustrate just how dramatic has been the change in the proportions of the budget spent on different areas of welfare in the past 50 years, and particularly over the last 20 years. Up until the Thatcher era contributory insurance payments grew in importance – from 55 per cent of the bill (at a time when a huge bill went on non-contributory war pensions which were rightly in payment, but which necessarily distorted the proportions spent under each head) up to 67 per cent in the last year of the Callaghan Government in 1978/9. By 1992 that position had so changed that only 49.5 per cent of the total budget went on insurance benefits, with 16.5 and 34 per cent on non-

Table 1.1 **Social security expenditure by benefit category**

Proportion of total spending on contributory, non-contributory non-means-tested and means-tested benefits – GB (figures rounded up/down)

	1948/9	1949/50	1978/79	1997/98
Contributory	55%	62%	67%	45%
Non contributory/ non–means–tested	31%	26%	16%	20%
Means tested	13%	13%	17%	35%
Total	100%	100%	100%	100%

Source: DSS Annual Reports; DSS Abstract of Statistics 1997.

contributory and means-tested benefits respectively. In a little over a decade, a national insurance based system (an approach which might well have appealed to a grocer's daughter) was replaced by one where most benefit payments were not linked to contributions. This is again a change that those considering Mrs Thatcher's beliefs would have thought highly improbable.

Thinking the unthinkable on the welfare budget centred on how to realign welfare's finances towards a much greater emphasis on benefit being earned. There was, however, a second reason why thinking the unthinkable concentrated attention on the dominant role means-testing was beginning to play.

Welfare and behaviour

While it was accepted that there would always be a role for means-testing, there was, I thought, agreement on two issues. First, while means-testing could not be phased out overnight, the welfare reform programme would ensure that at the end of the process fewer, rather than more, individuals and families would be dependent on means-tested welfare. Second, welfare expenditure affected how people behaved. The reform programme aimed at a reduced role for means-testing because this kind of welfare undermined the very behaviour that was central to the building of strong communities and the existence of a vibrant and honest society.

The reasons why post-war welfare in Britain originally laid down near-compulsory insurance coverage are disarmingly simple – so simple that they are sometimes forgotten. With everybody included within the national scheme, risks were spread over the widest possible base. Similarly, with near-universal coverage, life's freeloaders had to pay for the benefits they only too readily demanded. Moreover, the insurance principle was seen to support the normal behaviour of people wanting to work, and wishing to save, and in their desire not to be a burden on others. The idea of providing universal flat-rate minimum benefits, determined only by the contribution conditions, was that individuals and families could work at improving their own lot, and do so in a way that added to the general prosperity of the wider society. Insurance-based welfare therefore worked with the grain of human nature.

Means-tests on the other hand strike at the very heart of

this most basic settlement between Government and people. Means-tests penalise the very basis upon which a free and prosperous society depends. Means-tests take account of income. They therefore impose a penal tax on working, or on working harder. Means-tests take account of savings. They therefore impose a penal tax on savings. Means-tests depend on answers to questions about income and savings. They therefore impose a penal tax on honesty.

While any level of means-tested provision could have this impact on the actions of recipients, the concern about means testing becomes of a different order when every third pound of welfare is paid on a means-tested basis. Under the Tories the numbers of individuals living in households dependent on one or more means-tested benefits rose from 1 in 6 to 1 in 3 of the entire population.

There are a number of forces at work which account for the growing dominance of means-tested welfare. One is that insurance benefits are paid at a lower level than means-tested entitlement. People without other income or savings have to claim means-tested benefits to bring their income up to the minimum guaranteed by the state. In the words of Iain Macleod and Enoch Powell in 1951 – who were the first to comprehend what was happening:

> ...the wholly illogical position has now been reached that a compulsory universal insurance scheme provides a grant-in-aid towards the maintenance by national assistance under a means-test of those who lose other sources of income.[2]

Another reason was that past Governments saw extending means-tested help both as the least costly option and one which also concentrated help on the most vulnerable. Who, it was argued, could be against that dual proposition? It was when the longer-term consequences of means-tested help were brought into the equation that a much more considered answer was required.

An equally important and insidious reason for the growth in means-tested expenditure is that means-tested welfare teaches people the benefits of dishonesty and bad behaviour. Of course, for many people, means-tested benefits are a lifeline, rightly seized after what is often a long period of poorly paid employment. And other beneficiaries claim help and remain pure as the driven snow. But not all claimants by any means are in these categories. For them the rules are well known: do not work, and the state will look after you. Do not save, and the state will come to your rescue. Do not tell the truth, and the state will reward you with taxpayers' money. A dominance of means-tested welfare therefore strikes at the very heart of the idea of the good society of which welfare's original idealism was a crucial part.

Moreover, once individuals are on means-tested welfare they soon realise that they are trapped. Here is one of the major reasons why this part of the welfare bill expands inexorably. Disengaging from means-tested welfare is bad for your income. Indeed, in extreme cases, individuals trying to extricate themselves from means-tested welfare can find themselves being made worse off. Others face marginal tax rates on their effort of 50, 60, 70, 80 or 90 per cent – all rates above what is deemed unacceptable for those paying higher rate of income tax. Once on means-tested welfare the pressures work to keep people there. Instead of welfare acting as a springboard to freedom it becomes a trap to long-term dependency.

Means-tests fly in the face of duty-based welfare – of the kind spelt out clearly in chapter 11 of the Green Paper. Part of thinking the unthinkable in Opposition was that a major part of Labour's reform programme would be the creation of new benefits which people would earn, and from which all the signals would promote work, savings and honesty.

Unconditional welfare
The changing composition of the welfare bills – from financing the costs by way of insurance contributions to a growing reliance on taxed financed non-contributory benefits – was tracked by a transformation in the ideas the elite held about welfare. Indeed, it would have been surprising if the public language about welfare had not developed in order to help justify the dramatic financial basis on which welfare is built. From a starting position that welfare was earned by way of contributions, welfare was allowed to develop into a system based on rights linked to a rather vague concept of citizenship. This change in the language of welfare also reflected a fundamental shift in the nature of what welfare was perceived to be about. From the very rigorous concept of earning insurance cover, welfare developed into an altruistic act that was awarded unconditionally.

Thinking the unthinkable on this front asked why people needed welfare. Was it because society determined who would fail, and welfare was a compensation for failure? Or did individuals have some say in events and even some responsibility for what happened to themselves? The answers to both questions were important for they determined the nature of the welfare offered.

It is impossible to consider this side of the thinking the unthinkable debate without calling into court the ideas of Richard Titmuss. Titmuss, originally an insurance clerk, became one of the most talented and creative of social policy academics. The story of how his ideas spread, largely creating a new discipline, has yet to be told adequately. Two aspects of his thinking were of importance to the challenge made by the thinking the unthinkable exercise.

In opening up his academic career Titmuss rallied the troops to the view that poverty should be considered, not in terms of individual failure, but in structural terms. An individual was poor because he or she lived in a society where there were not enough jobs, or the jobs paid low wages, or the earnings from those jobs prevented workers saving for their old age. Poverty was not caused by personal inadequacy. An individual's actions and motivations were not relevant considerations.

By itself such views might be considered an interesting, if eccentric, part of the debate. Joined with another of Titmuss's premises, it produced a very different political cocktail. Titmuss believed that we were on the threshold of abundance: in 'an age of abundance of things, the production of consumption goods will become a subsidiary question for the West'.[3]

In this age of abundance, whatever the nature of welfare had been, it was transformed. Welfare could be delivered free of conditions and obligations. Judgments need not be made of those presenting themselves for help. Indeed, the lack of such judgments was central to Titmuss's belief on how universal welfare services could help establish a basic equality between individuals.

This belief in equality was the central, normative driving force in Titmuss's work. In setting this goal he followed the political tradition set by another Richard, in this case Tawney. Tawney's ideas about equality sprang from his views about the creation. Men and women are created in God's image. Their equality stems from this most basic of facts about their existence.

But Tawney accepted in total the Christian cosmology, not just the attractive parts of it. The nature of man was the putty which the reformers might try to fashion into a structure of great beauty. But that putty was stamped right through by man's fall. So while mankind had the possibility of being redeemed, and therefore of perfection, the only starting point for reformers was his fallen nature which was the characteristic in this world.

The Christian view of mankind led reformers to promote a different view of welfare from Centre-Left agnostics. Given the nature of man, it was unwise in most instances to provide welfare without conditions. Moreover, the age of abundance was still far off. Welfare was a scarce good. Given human nature, individuals were likely to respond more carefully if the benefits they were drawing had been earned and were not being presented as a free good.

Thinking the unthinkable on this front was about placing a Christian understanding of mankind centre stage. Understandably, though, no-one spoke in a Christian language which, far from being a conveyor of meaning, was fast becoming a barrier to understanding. But the policy followed from this analysis; welfare was returned to its status of being earned, and dependent on clear conditions being fulfilled before it was offered.

Similarly, the Christian view of human nature leads to a sceptical appreciation of the role altruism should play as a motive force underpinning welfare provision. For Titmuss welfare should be organised on a basis so that the human social and biological need to help others could be expressed through national institutions. In altruism Titmuss saw a major driving force both in supporting and shaping welfare.

For the Christian apologist a comparison with love and justice is here highly relevant. Love (altruism) might be expressed within small groups such as families or within very close friendships. But it was not a motive force on which the institutions of wider society could be safely governed. Here justice was the highest ideal on which human beings could operate.

That is not to say that altruism is not practised by individuals beyond the close group. Nor that the quality of life in the public domain is not raised when it is operated on this wider platform. For it clearly is. It is, rather, that such actions will necessarily be partial and inoperative over much of society for much of the time. Thinking the unthinkable therefore concerned two related issues. Welfare had to return to being a good which had to be earned and was conditional on a range of qualifications being fulfilled. And a clear distinction had to be made on the motive force in the most intimate of social groups, where altruism or love operated, and the more general and robust principles of justice on which welfare could operate in the wider society.

Universalism the goal

The fourth area where thinking the unthinkable occurred in Opposition was on the means by which universal provision of benefits could be maintained. Up until this point it had simply been assumed that, just as night followed day, universal provision was only possible through a state-run scheme. Thinking the unthinkable involved cutting this umbilical cord which tied the form of benefit to the means of its delivery.

The Left's response to the initial attempts to see universal benefits separately from the means of their delivery was one of extreme scepticism, if not outright opposition. For the Left, such a strategy was merely a clever ploy to destroy the universalism of the 1945 settlement. The very opposite was, of course, the case. Only by separating the need for universal provision from a state monopoly supply would it be possible in the future to extend the universal ideal. The attempt to find new ways of delivering universalism was not an isolated policy objective. It was a crucial part in building up a strategy where social inclusion moved beyond being merely a political slogan.

To think along these lines, of course, held dangers. Politicians might simply use the first part of the analysis, that universal provision should not be equated with state provision, to cut benefits and force people into the private market. But that was not then part of thinking the unthinkable.

The reality running through much of the revisionism was

an attempt to come to terms with the public's attitude to the payment of taxes and to the receipt of services. There was and is a resistance to the payment of taxes, yet there continues to be a demand for high-quality public services. Thinking the unthinkable was about trying to square what appeared to be two diametrically opposed circular forces.

A most fundamental change had taken place in the electorate's view on the payment of taxes. A number of factors were at work. The collapse of deference is in part responsible. The political elite's wisdom on what was good for the masses was not now allowed to pass without rigorous questioning from voters. More important, although perhaps they were linked, was the impact of rising national income. The Crosslandite view (and one I used to share) was that as national income rose, and with it real living standards, resistance to the payment of taxes would decline.

The opposite has in fact occurred. Rising living standards has increased the resistance to the tax take on incomes. Why? The answer is once again disarmingly simple. As real incomes have risen, so too have the choices open to individuals on how that income might be spent. And these are choices that individuals themselves increasingly want to make.

The idea that rising tax bills will be hidden by rising real wages has proved to be one of the great fallacies of the postwar period. Income levels now offer a growing body of voters the chance for the very first time to make major decisions themselves on the composition of their standard of living. Such opportunities are seized with relish.

Instead of merely railing against this change, thinking the

unthinkable was about accepting it as the framework within which the development of welfare should take place. The challenge for the Centre Left was how to make this provision of universal services compatible with this new set of voter preferences. New membership-run organisations would need to be on offer if voters were to forgo part of their current income to meet their own future welfare liabilities.

A key area concerns pensions. Not only is this the largest part of the budget, but so much of successfully implementing the fruits of thinking the unthinkable rested on getting in place a successful pensions reform.

That new thinking was the first attempted on the Centre Left back in 1993[4] by Matthew Owen and myself. The aim was to show how it was possible, with the restraint taxpayers now impose on policy makers, to achieve an adequate universal provision of pensions. The means to that end was to form a partnership with the private and mutual sectors. I stress the word partnership. Thinking the unthinkable was not then about how the state could cut and run on its responsibilities. Those first ideas have since been developed. But the objective of universal funded pensions is central to the whole development.

Welfare and democracy

The fifth area where thinking the unthinkable took place centred around the nature of civil society. This issue was not a semi-detached part of the reform agenda. It was and is intimately linked with how welfare affects behaviour and thereby character. It is crucially linked to how best to police welfare expenditure. It was also equally concerned with strengthening democracy at a time when the cry 'constitutional reform' was the rage.

Beveridge claimed that the social security system born out of his great report mysteriously grew up into an adult which in significant respects both shocked and displeased him. Beveridge may well have been both shocked and displeased with the outcome, but the welfare system we have today is very much governed by the genes which were implanted by his 1942 report.

What was so surprising was that Beveridge seemed willing to ignore so many of the lessons he had learned over the previous 40 years, in those early forays into society from his base at Toynbee Hall. Beveridge, like most of the great reformers of that period, such as the Webbs and the Bosanquets, was intrigued by the startling social advance made by so many of the skilled working class during the late Victorian and early Edwardian age. The mechanism of this success, and how it could be transmitted to other parts of the working class, was a key obsession with reformers.

Both Left and Right located the engine force of such social advance in the friendly society movement. The friendly societies were part of a self-help culture of the Victorian age and they prospered at a time when individuals genuinely believed that they could advance their own self-interest, and that of their neighbours, by joining together in voluntary associations. So why was it that Beveridge ended up making proposals which struck at the very basis of the self-help organisations in civil society?

In part Beveridge was hoisted by his own petard. His

committee was established merely to conduct a tidying-up operation across the social services. It was Beveridge who galvanised that body into one which produced a great report. But to make the case for revolutionary changes – for that is what Beveridge aimed to do – he was forced to draw a picture of the unhappy state of pre-war welfare. Much was then wrong. But Beveridge felt the need to exaggerate the problem with which he then set about dealing.

Crucial to his argument was the inadequacy of the coverage of friendly society schemes. Above all – so the charge sheet read – they had failed to ensure universal coverage. That Beveridge underestimated the effectiveness of these schemes is now becoming more appreciated. That a million fewer women had insurance coverage at the start of Beveridge's scheme in comparison with the pre-war status quo hints at a range of welfare coverage Beveridge knocked away in his bid, ironically, to provide that elusive universal provision.

Part of Beveridge's brilliance was to see the opportunity of presenting welfare reform as part of the post-war settlement, and as a prize to the nation for enduring the hardships that the fight against Nazism necessarily entailed. To build on the existing provision would have been a painstaking and slow process. Such an approach could not in any way have matched up to the propaganda bill Beveridge believed necessary. So the existing structure was to be swept away and a national system of benefits paid at a minimum level was to be introduced. As a sop to the old order Beveridge suggested that friendly societies should have a role in administering sickness benefit.

Beveridge replaced the friendly society administrator with the Government official. Beveridge replaced the voluntary organisation of welfare by a Government body. And Beveridge replaced the easy policing which came from individual friendly society officers knowing personally who was claiming benefit by little, if any, checks at all. The utopian belief was that people would not cheat their own schemes – as opposed to those run by private companies.

The trade unions acting, as they so often did, as friendly societies knew otherwise. Here is an example cited by Jose Harris of how tight a ship friendly societies insisted on operating.

In cases of fraud, however trivial, unions had no hesitation in bringing benefit swindlers before the court. 'The society had no vindictive feelings', reported the AST (the Amalgamated Society of Tailors and Tailoresses) in 1910 on the occasion of the prosecution of a sick member who had altered a benefit cheque for five shillings, 'but they felt that this was a matter which should be brought forward as a warning and deterrent against the committal of similar offences.' When this particular offender was sentenced to five months imprisonment with hard labour he was expelled from the society, 'we are well rid of such characters' was the comment in the Union's monthly report.[5]

Beveridge also believed that, by proposing minimum rates of benefit, a growing body of individuals would be encouraged to add a second tier of benefits based on voluntary contributions. Here he was wrong twice over. The minimum soon settled in the public mind as the maximum that they needed to provide for themselves. And, more importantly, because insurance benefits were soon paid at below the value of the assistance benefits, any additional individual coverage made the saver ineligible for the extra help on offer.

It is nevertheless important not to forget in the weighing of these reforms the advantage which Beveridge's scheme made for most contributors, and the way most contributors saw the scheme in those early days. There was considerable enthusiasm for the proposals which held out for the very first time the possibility of abolishing want. But, equally, it is important not to be blind to the downside of what amounted to the nationalisation of welfare. Beveridge, the great advocate of mutuality, and of self-help as a great engine force of social advance, proposed reforms which cut at the very root of the self-help membership organisations. More than any person this century, Beveridge laid bare a whole swathe of civil society.

The effect of this devastation is now apparent. Beveridge's welfare state has helped sap individual responsibility and initiative. It was no longer an individual's responsibility to look after himself and his family. It was the state's, once he had paid the necessary minimum contributions. And then, worse still, this attitude spread to how the other non-insurance benefits were viewed. They too became a right, even though no direct contributions had been paid to finance them.

Conclusion

Here I have introduced the five areas where thinking the unthinkable took place in Opposition. These five areas were not disparate initiatives. They were, in fact, part of building a new cohesive idea of welfare that would itself be part of the Government's wider objective for downsizing the state. That redefinition of the state was to be achieved by redrawing the boundary line between what should properly be undertaken by the individual and family, and which responsibilities could be safely left to the Government. Thinking the unthinkable was about changing the balance between these different motive forces governing society.

The thinking the unthinkable project was essentially a conservative one. It was about ensuring that the common decencies held by most people became once again the main stimulus of public policy. Thinking the unthinkable meant returning once again to those first principles that most of us still hold to be self-evident truths. Such an approach should not equate welfare reform with a mere trip down memory lane. Those spin doctors who pushed this line in the wake of my resignation merely illustrated either how little they understood, or how late they had come to the project, or indeed both.

Thinking the unthinkable involved accepting that the only sure foundation for welfare was to build on the natural impulses in most of us to look after ourselves and those that we most love. This aspect joined with other parts of the thinking the unthinkable project in seeing the danger means-tested provision poses to the operation of such decent impulses. Means-tests undermine the foundation of a self-help and family responsibility based approach, and makes those who behave decently feel foolish and taken for a ride by the more unscrupulous citizenry.

Thinking the unthinkable was therefore linked to ideas which pondered how best to transform the growing dominance of means-tested welfare. Labour was to inherit a welfare state, a great part of which acts as a ceiling over the head of most claimants, preventing them from making major changes to their own and their families' wellbeing by working, saving, and acting honestly. The quest was for a welfare state which acted as a springboard to freedom. Such a springboard could only be built if welfare provided a tier of help upon which individuals could build by their own efforts and not be penalised by so doing.

Rebuilding and repositioning civil society in the democratic life of the country also linked up with other parts of the thinking the unthinkable project. The growing resistance of voters to ever higher tax bills led to considering in what circumstances taxpayers would more enthusiastically meet their own future welfare liabilities. The growth of membership-run organisations, helping to provide overall a universal provision, was where thinking the unthinkable inexorably led on this issue.

Equally, thinking the unthinkable was part of the great debate on constitutional change. It is impossible to conceive of a democracy in which there is not universal suffrage. But having the vote alone does not make for a mature democracy. Both the representation of interests and the safeguarding of individual freedom require a flourishing civil society.

The rebuilding of these institutions which encompass more than individuals and families, but are less than the state, was also part of thinking the unthinkable. Indeed, for most English voters, that is by far and away the vast majority of the UK electorate, the rebuilding of such defences against an all too powerful Government, and the opportunities gained thereby for greater freedom, held more attraction than the seemingly endless debate on Scottish and Welsh devolution and the impending reform of the House of Lords.

Notes
* Lecture delivered to the Christendom Trust, 1 December, 1998.
1 See *Welfare Reform Focus Files*, for details of expenditure and trends for separate benefits, DSS, 1997.
2 *The Social Services: Needs and Must*, CPC, 1952, p.35-6
3 cited in Deacon, 'Richard Titmuss: Twenty Years On', *Journal of Social Policy*, Vol 22, April 1993, 237.
4 Frank Field and Matthew Owen, *Private Pensions for All: Squaring the Circle*, Fabian Society, 1993. Also their *National Pensions Savings Plan: Universalising Private Pension Provision*, Fabian Society, 1994.
5 'Victorian Values and the Founders of the Welfare State' in *Proceedings of the British Academy*, 78, 1992, p.176.

3. The Eye of the Storm*

After nearly three years of the life of this Government it is now possible to discuss the nature and direction of its welfare reform programme. Here I wish to set out what I see as that approach, and the values that underpin it.

An FT view of the world
Not for the first time Nicholas Timmins in the *Financial Times* puts into print what I believe the Government subscribes to in private.[1] Let me present the kernel of Timmins's argument.

> Universalism in Britain's welfare state is dying ... The old concept of a welfare state was one in which, very broadly, everyone paid taxes and everyone drew benefits, many of them regardless of income. That has been fractured by widening income inequality and rising cost. It is never to be repaired.

The irony of what he believes to be happening is not lost on Timmins.

> Universalism in social security is dying, paradoxically at the hands of the party that has historically been its biggest champion – the Labour party. Its death throes can be dated: they began with the former prime minister

Jim Callaghan's 'monetarist' speech to the Labour party conference in October 1979 and ended with Frank Field's resignation as Minister for Welfare Reform in July of last year.

The former marks the moment when, for reasons only partially connected with policies of successive Labour and Conservative Governments, income inequality started to widen dramatically in the UK. The latter marks the departure of the one minister in the present Government who was committed to rebuilding universalism, albeit not through the route of traditional state benefits.

The *Financial Times* article carried what the Government wishes the country to believe about its strategy. Universalism was being abandoned so as to free the Government to redistribute to the poor on a scale to warm the hearts of even the most cynical political commentators. Redistribution is taking place not only from rich to poor but from the childless to those with children.

Timmins did consider the political risks attached to this strategy. What, he wondered, would be the political fallout when the penny dropped and the middle class woke up to the extent of their loss of universal social security provision? Would their anxieties be assuaged by the £40 billion additional funding going into the two areas which most concern them – schools and the NHS?

Here I wish to consider three key questions arising from what we now know about the Government's strategy.

59

- First, what are the dimensions of widening the income inequality which has given rise to the overthrow of universalism as a key part of Labour strategy?
- Second, what resources has the Government so far committed in the opposite direction to counter widening income inequality?
- And third, is the approach of redistributing through means-testing not part of the problem rather than part of the solution?

First, a few facts about the widening inequality in earnings and incomes in Britain.

Countering growing income inequality

Peter Lilley was the first senior British politician to try and centre the debate on the causes, rather than simply the consequences of a growing inequality in earnings.[2] Indeed what Lilley was at pains to stress was that widening earnings inequalities were not unique to Britain. According to him they had 'occurred across the developed world'.[3] The inference was clear. While Conservative Governments since 1979 had made quite staggering changes in the distribution of the tax burden – from richer onto poorer people – the main dynamics of income inequality were to be found in changes in the economy.

The two movements – of Government policy and worldwide economic forces – were not, however, quite as distinct as ministers then wished us to believe. The Government's Exchange Rate policy in the early 1980s was responsible for destroying one in three manufacturing jobs in this country in almost as many years. Many of these jobs were moderately well paid and most were held by men. Their destruction helped shift the distribution of income, as millions of male wage earners fell down the income scale to become unemployed heads of households living on benefit levels of income.

Similarly, the process of deregulation, which went far beyond the financial services sector, had a major impact on opening up the economy to greater international competitiveness than many of our competitors, and to the very forces generating greater income inequality to which Peter Lilley first drew attention. The message was a clear one; and one that now brings to mind Bill Clinton's election campaign rhetoric of 1992. It's the economy, stupid, which was and is the main driving force in determining the dispersion of income; although, stupid, Government action was pivotal in deciding the extent of the free play which would be given to these same economic forces.

Widening inequality

Whatever the cause, the extent of the widening gulf in income between the top and bottom of British society is undisputed. From 1979 and up until 1995 to 1997 average real income grew by a little over 40 per cent. This growth was not, however, evenly spread. The poorest 10 per cent saw their income rise by 12 per cent (it actually fell by 9 per cent after taking into account housing costs) while at the other end of the scale, the richest 10 per cent saw their incomes surge by 62 per cent (70 per cent after taking into account housing costs).[4]

Differential changes in income growth on this scale have, not surprisingly, affected the shares of income going to the various income groups. The top 10 per cent saw each share of total income rise from 21 to 27 per cent, while the poorest 10 per cent saw their share of income halved from 4 to 2 per cent.

Collectively the richest 10 per cent saw their disposable income rise by approximately £48 billion during this period. In household terms this meant rises, in 1998 prices, of £160 a week for a married couple – significantly more than the £103 basic state pension on offer to a retired couple last year; and £267 a week for a couple with three children – an increase equal to almost twice last year's income support benefit for a similar sized family.

So let me now turn to that second question which I posed at the start. What has been the pattern and extent of Governmental redistribution so far enacted by the Labour Government against the backdrop of an unprecedented shift of resources to the rich?

It is important to stress that the widening dispersion of earnings, which has been used as the rationale for dropping a universalist approach to welfare, has occurred over a decade and a half. On all counts therefore one would expect the degree of counter-redistribution over the first two years of the Government's life to be modest in comparison with the work of economic forces over the last decade and a half.

Redistribution

The Government has extended what legitimately should be thought of as a redistributory strategy. Work rather than benefit generally leads to a higher income. So, as well as considering traditional fiscal and benefit changes, attention should be focused on the Government's welfare to work strategy. £5 billion was raised from the privatised utilities to pursue this major initiative, the long-term consequences of which will, I believe, have a major impact in transforming what is commonly thought of as welfare provision.

The main social security changes can be considered under three board categories. There are first those changes which reduced the income of people claiming benefit.

These include:

- A reduction in the time limit to one month for claiming social security benefits.
- The abolition of the lone parent rate of child benefit in respect of the eldest child.
- A reduction in lone parent premium in income-related benefits.

In total these three changes cut the income of some of the poorest families by about £200 million a year.

The second group of changes consists of reforms which clearly help the poor although, as I will argue in a moment, the 'cost' is way beyond that listed in the public expenditure accounts. Two reforms centre on giving additional income to pensioners. The winter fuel bonus saw some redistribution to the poorest pensioners on income support, who gained £50 a year bonus per household, with the bulk of the expenditure, of £20 bonuses, spread evenly throughout the rest of the pensioner population. (The scheme has since been revised to give all pensioner households a £100 winter fuel bonus.)

The pension guarantee, ensuring all pensioners with only nominal savings will raise the weekly income of the poorest pensioners to a new minimum level, and channels an additional £265m a year to this group (460,000 pensioners are left below the guaranteed income level because the notional income derived from their savings makes them ineligible for income support).

Families with children have benefited by the following reforms.

- An increase in the means-test benefit rate by £2.50 a week for children under 11.
- The introduction of the working families tax credit which is specifically targeted to a million families with children will ensure that such families gain on average £17.20 a week, costing an additional £2.5 billion in a full financial year.
- A child benefit increase for the first child of £2.50 a week from April of this year and costing £875 million in a full year.

A third group of reforms will protect the poorest while at the same time stripping out support for all other families and individuals, including those on modest incomes. The changes being proposed to widow's and disability benefits will result in a net reduction in benefit payments of £1.3 billion. The vast majority of those set to lose from the changes to incapacity benefit entitlement, for example, are in the bottom 40 per cent of income distribution.[5] Practically the whole of this group will become solely dependent on means-tested assistance.

No simple pattern therefore emerges in considering the winners and losers in the Government's welfare reforms. There hasn't been a clear redistribution to the poor away from the rich, nor simply to children at the cost of the childless. The picture is much more complex.

The much welcomed increase in child benefit for the first child has largely been paid for by a substantial reduction in the married person's tax allowance. A sizeable proportion of the cost of the child benefit increase is therefore being borne by families with children who have seen their tax burden increase in line with the reduction of the married person's tax allowance.

Other reforms, such as the winter fuel bonus, have been weighted in value towards the poor, but most of the expenditure has gone to other pensioner households.

There are, also, two further sets of reforms affecting the poor. There have been those, such as the introduction of an income support pensioner guarantee, which has targeted help exclusively on the poorest.

There have been other reforms too, which have not resulted in additional income going to the poor, but which have insured that the income of this group has not fallen at a time when support was being stripped away from all other individuals and households. Reform to widow's and incapacity benefits are prime examples here.

But under the new contract the poor will generally only gain help on the basis of a means-tested programme. And it is the cumulative impact of adding yet more people to the means-tested welfare rolls which I believe represents the greatest danger for the Government's welfare reform strategy. Here the debate moves on to the last question I wish to consider. Is this drive to ever greater means-testing part of the problem, rather than the solution to the welfare conundrum?

The firm smack of human nature

Universalism is seen by the Government as increasingly irrelevant as a means of countering growing income inequality. Targeting, or means-testing, is largely the order of the day. But because this strategy takes no account of how means-tests impact on human behaviour the Government's approach is likely to compound rather than relieve the extent of poverty.

One part of thinking the unthinkable in Opposition was to accept that welfare impacts on human nature and that human nature responds to the kind of welfare offered. Before the election I described the continual drive of poorer people on to means-tested assistance as a state-run war of attrition against self-improvement.

The Tories are still roundly and rightly condemned by the Labour Government for doubling the numbers on means-tested assistance: up from 1 in 6 to 1 in 3 of the population. The reason for this condemnation is simple. Means-tests penalise three of the cardinal virtues which act as the warp and weft of a vibrant and civilised society: of work, saving and honesty.

Yet the Government has now embarked on a strategy

similar to that employed by the Tories. Let me illustrate by way of its approach to pensioner poverty why I believe its policy will be self-defeating.

The Government has published plans for the long-term reform of pensions. The aim is to increase the numbers of people saving for their own retirement as well as to raise the amount that such individuals regularly place in pension schemes.

At the same time the Government has announced its intention of introducing a pension guarantee for existing pensioners. This guarantee will be set at £75 a week and £116.60 a week respectively for single and married pensioners. The guarantee will therefore be worth £8 more than the single person's state pension and £9.90 more than the married couples' retirement pension. (The difference currently stands at £10.95 for a single pensioner and £14.05 for a married couple.)

The pension guarantee is in fact a re-badging of the existing income support arrangements for pensioners. As well as being worth therefore an additional £429 a year for a single pensioner (the difference between the state retirement pension's value and the new pensioner income guarantee) income support brings with it an automatic eligibility to a range of what are called passport benefits. Housing benefit is worth on average about £2,000 a year to a pensioner, and council tax benefit comes in at about £420 a year. Other benefits, such as free dental treatment, which is also a right of income support claimants, brings the value of this additional package, over and above the value of the state retirement pension, to around £3,000 per year.

Any pensioner with an additional pension of less than this amount, or savings which generate less than that level of income, are automatically made poorer. An estimate gained from the Government by Steve Webb MP is that an additional £41,000 savings will now be required to give a pensioner an income that is just a penny more than he would have had had he not saved and instead had chosen simply to rely on all means-tested assistance available.

But of course the position in real life is far worse than these figures suggest. The penalty on savings is clear. An individual needs to save substantially more than £41,000 – so that that their income is reasonably above the means-tested standard of living. For example, who in their right mind wants to, let alone can, save £41,000 only to be 50p a week better off?

If amassing substantial savings is not a realisable possibility, then the only reasonable alternative course of action is not to save at all, to raise today's living standard by spending the whole of one's income, and to rely on means-tested assistance in retirement. An alternative scenario might be to save, but to do so in a way in which it makes it difficult for authorities to track down the savings and the income gained thereby.

From poverty trap to poverty chasm

Back in 1971 the phrase 'poverty trap' was coined.[6] This phrase was to highlight a new phenomenon whereby the interaction of tax and the loss of eligibility for the newly introduced means-tested family income supplement could result in workers not getting what they bargained for.[7] A pay increase could result not in an overall increase in disposable income, but an actual fall in net income.

The poverty trap no longer adequately describes the position in which millions of pensioners and future pensioners now find themselves. Income support entitlement, and the new pension guarantee, have passport rights attached to them. The poverty trap still bites. A small occupational pension can leave pensioners up to £3,000 a year worse off than they would have been had they not been members of a pension scheme, or ensured that they had not saved. But in respect of savings, the value of the passported benefits now creates a poverty chasm. The message is clear. Do not bother saving if you cannot amass substantially more than £41,000.

But how many people on modest earnings can expect to have already amassed this sizeable capital? The size of this chasm is already such that most people know they will not be able to jump clear and establish a capital sum which will lead to a standard of living well in excess of the means-tested level.

Worse still, this poverty chasm is set ever to widen. This is what I mean by the Government dynamising the whole problem. The Government is pledged to index the pension guarantee to earnings. The state retirement pension is indexed to prices only. Occupation pensions may be linked at best to modest price rises, and falling interest rates on savings and consequently annuities are set to dive to an all time low. The pensions guarantee will therefore cumulatively outstrip other pension income year by year.

If wages continue to rise over the next 20 years as they have over the last two decades, then the savings needed to guarantee an income in retirement 1p above the guaranteed minimum will not be £40,000 but £100,000.

This, then, is the message now going out to all middle-aged workers. Don't bother saving. Saving but failing to meet the £100,000 target will result in you being penalised in two ways. You will first be accepting a much lower standard of living now in order to save. But, second, you will then be penalised for behaving properly by having a pension income lower than that which is gained by right by other people who have not bothered to save. To those beginning their working career, the message about the amount of saving now required for a self-reliant retirement is even more stark.

Should any of Britain's poorest third of citizenry currently call upon a financial adviser, the advice they should receive is clear. Don't save. You can only damage your financial health by doing so. Similarly, the message they will be given, sadly, is: don't join a pension scheme as it is unlikely to make you better off in retirement. Indeed, it may leave you considerable worse off.

And because the pension guarantee is linked to earnings, the savings chasm is set to widen, causing this third of the population to grow. Yet this growing catastrophe has been bought on the cheap. The cost of the pension guarantee is put by the Government at a mere £265 million a year – the equivalent of only 0.6 per cent of the entire social security budget spent on pensioners and a mere 0.3 per cent of the overall budget. Rarely can such potential economic and moral havoc have been purchased at such a modest price.

Not only are future pensioners affected by the Government's drive towards means-tested assistance. Once their income is above the means-tested eligibility level, all working class families are being affected by similar policies.

Insurance benefit coverage is being stripped out, leaving means-tested support only for those on the lowest income. In addition, the Government has stated its intention of replacing child benefit for over 16 year olds with a means-tested maintenance allowance. Furthermore, the payment of higher education fees, and the size of student loans, will shortly be determined on the basis of parental income.

All of these reforms will stretch to breaking point those modest budgets which have historically been used to help advance a whole generation of working class children.

Conclusion

Increasingly Britain is dividing into three major groups. First, there are those who have been driven into means-tested help. Second, there are those who, thank goodness, are well able to look after themselves. But I would suggest that there is, in addition, a third or so of the entire population who have incomes which exclude them from means-tested help, but who are in no way financially well placed.

It is this group which holds the key to social advance in any community. It is by their efforts that countries are marked either by advance or decay. It was to this very same group that Mrs Thatcher targeted so much attention. But the targeting then was rather different to that which is now occurring.

The Thatcher strategy was one of rewards – council house sales, and tax cuts. The Thatcher targeting resulted in a major haemorrhage of the traditional Labour vote. This haemorrhage was only finally reversed with Tony Blair's election as leader of the Labour Party.

It is this group of traditional working class families, and not the middle class cited by the *Financial Times* article, which will feel most keenly the full effect of the Government's welfare reform programme. For it is they who are now being asked to save at least £100,000 to have a dignified, self-reliant retirement, while simultaneously watching those benefits that have historically acted as incentives to better themselves – such as child benefit for children over 16 and free higher education – become a thing of the past. The result, of course, will be discouragement, as these generally industrious, aspirant people realise how small the margin has become between the rewards for their efforts and those lower down the ladder on benefit. Equally, discouragement will afflict those on benefit as they realise the size of the chasm they now have to jump to gain the firm ground of self-reliance.

It is the reaction of this group – the C1s and C2s – which should most concern a Labour Government. For it is this group who have proved to be the most volatile in terms of party loyalty over the past quarter of a century. Should they find a suitable vehicle through which to express their puzzlement, anger and disdain at how the Government's welfare reform programme is increasingly affecting them, the political consequences are impossible to predict.

But one thing is likely in any such fallout. For the Government and its supporters their ride will be anything but fun.

Notes

★ Leeds Chaplaincy Sermon given on 25 February, 1999.
1 Timmins, N., *Financial Times*, 10 February, 1999.
2 'The dispersion of earnings power and its consequences', in *Winning the Welfare Debate*, Social Market Foundation, 1995.
3 Ibid., p.28.
4 House of Commons Library, Statistical Section.
5 Hansard, 16 November 1999, c397w.
6 Field, F., & Piachaud D., 'The Poverty Trap', in the *New Statesman*.
7 FIS is the precursor of today's family credit which is itself soon to be relaunched as the working families tax credit.

4. Welfare in the Age of Low Taxation: the Role of National Insurance in Securing a National Minimum*

Marx once recalled how Hegel had somewhere asserted that all great events and personalities in world history reappear in one fashion or another and added that such events and personalities do so the first time around as tragedy and the second as farce. The advent of British national insurance proves an exception to this rule. Its start was anything but tragic. And far from being a farce second time around, events now appear to be set on tragedy.

National insurance was born in Britain at a time when British politicians were searching for the means by which to extend welfare without increasing taxes. The relevance to today's agenda hardly needs stressing. But equally Britain, as opposed to Germany, which already had a graduated national system of insurance, went for a flat-rate system of benefit. The British objective was to cover the weak. The Germans saw the system of graduated benefits as appealing to strong and more prosperous workers.

So were set two lasting characteristics of British social

security. Flat-rate benefits have generally proved the more sustainable and endurable. The aim has been to establish a national minimum. And its financing through national insurance has been viewed not as a tax but, coming on the back of the friendly societies' and trade union movement's welfare state, as an insurance payment.

Here I wish to touch on five themes.

- How British and German social security advanced in the face of obstacles to raising taxes.
- How there is in Britain today an even greater resistance to tax increases than there was at the turn of the century.
- How today's attitudes to national insurance are similar to those thought to have existed ninety years ago.
- How, ironically, given the Chancellor of the Exchequer's wish to sustain a 10p starting rate of tax, he should see insurance as an enemy to be destroyed.
- How insurance fits the Prime Minister's wish to counter the something-for-nothing society.

In the beginning

In true British style the advent of national insurance in this country came only after a 25-year campaign denigrating the German system which had been up and running since the 1880s. Leading politicians of all parties viewed developments in Germany with, at best, disapproval and, at worst, contempt. Insurance-based welfare was determinedly rejected at first in Britain, even though this rejection put new and expanding financial pressures on the Treasury.

When the Liberal Government of Campbell Bannerman,

with Asquith as Chancellor, began planning the introduction of the national system of old-age pensions, a major aim was to keep the cost to a minimum. Rather than aiming at a comprehensive scheme which would eradicate poverty in old age, a primary objective was to offer a scheme which would take the wind out of the sails of the national campaign for old-age pensions. But to keep the scheme within the Treasury's imposed cash ceiling of £6 million, the pension had to be limited to people of 70 or more, of good character, not in receipt of the Poor Law, and on modest income. It was an unstable compromise.

Lloyd George, who became Chancellor when the Government was reconstituted, with Asquith as Prime Minister, was aware that the national campaign would be calling for further concessions, with a reduction in the pension age to 65, or even 60, as a paramount target. The case for such a move was powerful. The average life expectancy of men was 48 years. Indeed as Liberal MPs commented at the time, with the 70-year threshold and a full contributory record being required, few if any would survive to make a full claim.

Lloyd George's departure to Germany in August 1908 to see the German insurance system for himself was therefore 'a turning point'. But it was a turning point with a difference. Professor Hennock explains that the reason for the trip was not one of simply reproducing the German insurance system here. Lloyd George:

> had heard enough to recognise that the so-called
> German invalidity insurance provided an alternative to

massive Treasury commitments and to an indiscriminate lowering of the pension age[1].

It was, then, the German means of financing welfare which was followed, not the shape of their benefit system. The German Reich 'possessed no power of direct taxation … therefore, an ambitious policy of meeting working class aspirations out of direct taxation was out of the question'[2]. Likewise in Britain, the development of welfare beyond non-contributory old-age pensions was a conscious decision by the Cabinet to construct its social policy 'according to its own priorities', rather than simply yielding to outside pressure. The introduction of compulsory insurance offered the prospect of moderating the impact growing welfare bills would otherwise have had on taxation [3].

There was also another objective at stake. The Liberal Government's intention was to keep the structure of welfare one stage removed from the state. That, after all, reflected the Liberal view of the proper role of the state and the part civil societies should play in the emerging democracy. The financing of British health insurance reflected the German scheme, but the means by which health services were to be delivered was grafted on to the British friendly society structure. And while there was much effort by Lloyd George to convince himself that the British scheme was in advance of the German model, British innovation came only in extending insurance to unemployment. This was a task not yet embarked upon by the Germans, but was advanced by Churchill as he took the Government into what he described as 'the untrodden field of politics'. [4]

Current barriers to increasing taxes

When Lloyd George was pondering the basis on which Britain's 20th century welfare should be built, the working class did not pay income tax. And that remained the position until the financing of World War Two brought most workers into the tax system. Insurance payments therefore had a threefold advantage to the Welsh Wizard:

- They would be in keeping with the friendly society culture of self-improvement and advance, and, initially, would ensure the strengthening of self-governing organisations.[5] This, in itself, was reflected in the wider political culture of the respective roles of state and individual.
- Insurance payments would, by making costs transparent, also act as a natural brake on both the continuous demand to improve welfare coverage, and the continuous demand to enhance the value of benefits.
- An insurance-based welfare scheme would prove the best way of checking abuse, as workers would be running their own schemes and would move swiftly to counter cheating. As an explanatory Memorandum to the National Insurance Bill stated: 'a purely State Scheme ... would inevitably lead to unlimited shamming and deception.[6]

While the issue of taxation remains central in today's political debate it does so in different circumstances from those which Lloyd George confronted. Then, as opposed to now, no-one in the working class paid income tax. The position confronting a Government today with almost universal payment of direct taxation can be expressed thus: the electorate appears wary of voting for tax increases, despite what they may say to pollsters outside the confines of the polling booth. At best they might vote for tax increases linked to specific objectives outlined by the Government which had won their confidence to spend wisely and carefully.

Why is it that, as real incomes rise, resistance to income tax does not fall? During the 1960s and early part of the 1970s I believed that it would become easier, not harder, to raise taxes as people became more prosperous. The answer to this apparent puzzle is, I fear, rather simple.

There is little evidence that people ever liked paying tax – as opposed perhaps to other groups paying tax on their behalf, e.g. working class attitudes to income tax paid largely by middle and upper groups up until 1940. More important has been the impact of rising national income on choice.

Taxation could be maintained in the early post-war period on the basis of a ratchet effect – taxes stayed at the level required to finance the war, and people simply accepted the status quo. And, more importantly, the services bought by taxes, such as health and education, could not be purchased individually.

This position is now less true, and becomes ever less so. It is as though there is a second stage to Engels' Law. That law, as you may remember, stipulates that, at a certain point of rising income, the proportion of that income spent on food begins to fall. Now it would appear that, in Western societies, there is a second threshold where rising income allows a real trade-off between tax-financed goods and individual purchases.

And the range of services is not only between state-provided and market-led substitutes, but between the whole range of customer purchases of homes, furnishings, holidays, and, increasingly, lifestyle consumption goods. Rising living standards, far from lessening any resistance to paying tax, let alone embracing a higher level, has made the demand for lower direct tax levels almost irresistible.

National Insurance and the 10p rate of tax
The Chancellor of the Exchequer's introduction of a 10p starting rate of tax not only fits with the overwhelming public wish to see lower direct taxation, but correctly judges a deeper issue of motivation. Most of the criticism of this move to a 10p starting rate centred on an opportunity cost analysis of how poorer workers would have been helped more with a tax allowance increase costing the same amount (although it is noticeable how quickly such negative comments subsided once the move had been announced). No-one should doubt the figures. For each set amount of money to reduce the tax burden, lowest paid workers gained more from increases in tax allowances, thereby raising the tax threshold, than by the introduction of a lower starting rate of tax.

What the figures do not show is how lower paid workers react once in work[7]. In 20 years as an MP I have never had a constituent talk about his or her average rate of tax. What is regularly and forcibly expressed to me is how much income is lost as extra effort – normally in working overtime – is taken by the taxman. It is at this point that the 10p starting rate of tax comes into its own. And the pressure will continue for the 10p band to be widened to cover an ever greater proportion of taxable income.

What is so surprising is that the Chancellor, who has judged this issue so accurately, now looks as though he will swamp this low tax bridgehead by the largely unstated, and I guess ill-thought through, national insurance reforms. On a number of occasions the Chancellor has referred to national insurance contributions as a tax. At the same time he has aligned the tax and national insurance threshold with national insurance contributions kicking in at a 10p rate.

Why aligning the tax and national insurance threshold was thought desirable has never been explained. It has been presented as a self-evident truth. It appeals, I suppose, to the tidy mind. While tidiness may be a virtue for a bureaucrat, it is likely to prove less attractive in the workplace. Aligning tax and national insurance rates, and calling national insurance contributions a tax, transforms at a stroke the starting rate of tax from 10p to 20p. The more often it is stressed by the Government that national insurance is a tax, the less meaningful the 10p starting rate of tax becomes.

Ironically, although the Chancellor sees national insurance contributions as a tax, taxpayers do not.[8] And we have only to look at the record of the last Conservative Government to see how successful it was in exploiting this particular reserve of public perception.

The last Government regularly increased national insurance contributions so as to give it room to reduce income tax. While overall the amount of tax raised from incomes and its proportion of GDP rose, the starting points of tax were reduced – often dramatically. At the same time the rates of national insurance were increased.

The result can be summarised by looking at a single person, a working married couple and a married couple with two children, all on average earnings, over the period of the Tory Government. Special emphasis is paid to the amount taken in tax and the size of the national insurance contributions.

In 1979 a single person on average earnings saw a quarter of their pay taken in income tax. By the end of the Tory regime it had fallen to 18.8 per cent. But national insurance contributions had increased by more than two percentage points – up from 6.5 per cent to 8.8 per cent.

For the married couple who were both working, but without children, the income tax take fell from 13 per cent of their average earnings to 12.4 per cent. National insurance contributions rose from 6.5 to 7.5 per cent.

A married couple with two children, on the average wage, saw their income tax take fall from 19.9 per cent of earnings to 17.5 per cent. But the national insurance contributions were pushed up from 6.5 per cent to 8.8 per cent of earnings over the period of the last Conservative Governments.

So, while the Conservatives continued to reap electoral rewards from being seen as a tax-cutting party, most taxpayers saw the proportion of income taken in tax and national insurance contributions rise. But because the rise was concentrated on increasing national insurance contributions, few, if any taxpayers believed or, more importantly, voted on the assumption that the Tories were a tax-raising party.

The perception of national insurance benefits being earned remained intact, despite the fact that higher contributions were accompanied by major cuts in entitlement. The four most significant moves on this front by Conservative Administrations were:

- abolition of the earnings-related supplements to unemployment and sickness pay;
- abolition of national insurance sick pay;
- halving the length of entitlement for what was called unemployment benefit and is now re-named the jobseeker's allowance;
- halving and then halving again entitlement from SERPS.

The present Government is continuing the process of reining back national insurance cover:

- IB is to be affluence-taxed with 50p of benefit withdrawn for each pound of pension payments over £85 a week;[9]
- eligibility to IB is to be cut from a year's contribution over a working life, to a minimum number of paid contributions in one of the last three tax years;
- the widow's pension for older women will be abolished.

On each occasion in the past, as with the current proposals, when national insurance entitlement has been cut a few high-profile extensions to benefit have been simultaneously announced. But these changes amount to very small beer when compared to the size of the cuts being made.

Voters' views on national insurance

The continuing popularity of national insurance comes from individual testimony as well as from a recently commissioned study by the DSS.

From letters I have received protesting about the Government's proposed cuts to national insurance coverage, individuals see their participation in the NI scheme in exactly the same way as they would membership of a friendly society or private scheme of insurance. Men in their 50s write of the contributions they have made for 30 or so years to ensure that, among other things, their wives would be covered by a widow's pension should they die early. National insurance contributions were happily made, and such contributions made contributions to a private scheme offering the same benefits unnecessary. The question often posed in these letters is how a Government can miss-sell the national insurance scheme in this way when private firms are rightly criticised by the same Government for giving wrong advice to customers. It is a question which remains unanswered.

The small-scale study undertaken for the DSS consisted in questioning eight discussion groups about their knowledge and perceptions of national insurance. The author remarked that 'Most of the respondents ... saw (their national insurance contributions) as a financial transaction, which gave them entitlement to a range of insurance benefits.[10] The study found that, far from support for national insurance dwindling, 'there was widespread support for extending the scope of national insurance to certain groups, notably carers, and to pay at least some benefits to those with an incomplete contribution record'.[11] Respondents believed 'that considerable savings [to meet the cost of extending coverage] could be achieved by reducing the level of fraud within the system.'[12]

The something-for-nothing society

The latest twist in the undermining of national insurance comes from the most surprising of sources. In selling the latest round of welfare reform to *Daily Mail* readers the Prime Minister declared a war on the something-for-nothing society.[13]

Practically everyone in the country sympathises with the Prime Minister's wish to ensure that those who can work should do so. A huge and ambitious welfare to work programme is underway for which the Government deserves both credit and support. But dependency for some people is an honourable estate. For people at the end of their working lives, and others for whom life has dealt the most difficult hand of cards, dependency is a badge of full citizenship awarded by a civilised community. Headline-making attacks on the dependency culture amongst those who are able-bodied, and who could work, but do not (or claim benefits while they are working) is a proper part of a political armoury.

The Prime Minister's crusade against the something-for-nothing society comes as he commends to the electorate a welfare bill which undermines the very idea that welfare should be earned.[14] For that is what the proposed cuts in national insurance coverage amount to. And such cuts are in contradiction of the clear promise in the Welfare Reform Green Paper *New ambitions for our country: A New Contract for Welfare*. Let me cite the text approved by the whole Cabinet.

> The development of the contract will lead to greater ... *trust* – with a clearer contract, people can have greater confidence that they will get proper protection in return for the contributions they make.[15]

If the Welfare Reform and Pensions Bill goes through unamended, one of the results will be the opposite of what the Prime Minister intends. Some people who have earned benefit coverage by past national insurance contributions will lose that entitlement. If that loss results in a claimant being reduced to a very low income, individuals may be eligible for means-tested assistance. But so too will those who have failed for whatever reason to earn a national insurance entitlement. Under the Bill no one from this latter group will lose any entitlement whatsoever. Loss of entitlement is reserved for the ranks of those who have earned and paid national insurance contributions. So far from an attack on the something-for-nothing society, the Bill is an attack on the something-for-nothing society.

Conclusions

The national insurance scheme was originally introduced because of tax restraints faced by the then Liberal Government. Following the German precedent, where the Federal Government had no powers to levy income tax and therefore adopted a contributory insurance scheme in order to finance an expanding welfare programme, the Liberal Government introduced British national insurance so that the pressures of an expanding welfare programme would not be met by direct taxation.

The present Labour Government was elected on a programme which included the promise not to increase direct taxation. It was a crucial commitment in convincing the electorate that Labour would not be profligate with taxpayers' money. But the demand for increases in collective welfare continue, and in these circumstances most Governments would see the attraction of building on the current insurance system – although of course the range of benefits and the grounds for eligibility need reform.

The unexpected irony is that the Chancellor views national insurance as a tax and apparently wishes to merge it with the income tax system. Yet success on this front will destroy the Government's attempt to establish a 10p starting rate of tax as a major tax band. It even brings into question whether in a merged tax and national insurance system anyone will believe tax begins at 10p at all.

An added irony comes from the fact that the Prime Minister wishes to slay the 'something-for-nothing society'. Yet the Government is simultaneously commending a Bill to Parliament which attacks the very basis of a something-for-something society. All the major cuts in welfare entitlement in the current welfare reform bill are aimed at individuals who have full contribution records to the scheme. In total the bill proposes to cut national insurance benefits to the tune of £1.3 billion for contributors who may have paid over 30 or more years for these benefits. In stark contrast not one penny is being taken away from claimants who draw benefits for which they have paid no direct contributions at all.

Notes

* ★ Speech given to the Manchester Securities Institute on 13 May, 1999.
1. E. P. Hennock 'The Origins of British National Insurance and the German Precedent', in *The Emergence of Welfare States in Britain and Germany*, ed. by W J Mommsen, Croom Helm, 1981, 86.
2. E. P. Hennock, *British Social Reform and German Precedents*, Oxford, 1987, 208.
3. loc. cit. 86.
4. W. S. Churchill, *Nation*, 7 March, 1908.
5. Although, sadly, this ideal did not survive the Committee Stage of the Bill in the Commons.
6. Hennock, 'The origins of British National Insurance and the German Precedent', 99.
7. Most of the public debate over the past three decades has centred, understandably enough, on the incentive gap of moving from benefit to work. It was, after all, a period during which the age of full employment seemed as though it had been blown away. And benefits were then a higher proportion of average earnings than they are now.
8. Bruce Stafford, *National Insurance and the Contributory Principle*, Social Security Research, DSS, 1998, 20.
9. The £85 figure will, hopefully, rise before the Act comes into force.
10. Stafford, 20.
11. op. cit. 38.
12. op. cit. 39.
13. *Daily Mail*, 10 February, 1999.

14 The Bill, after much parliamentary opposition, was given Royal Assent on 11 November, 1999.
15 Cmnd 3805, paragraph 11.6.

5. T. S. Eliot's View of Human Nature and the Debate on Welfare*

The Idea of a Christian Society has little direct relevance to the debate today about charity, let alone welfare, the two topics about which I have been asked to talk. The three essays that make up this book[1] are more than difficult to read. While Eliot gently boasts that as a poet he pays particular attention to the meaning of words, the sentences into which these words are spun often have a meaning which is difficult to fathom.

Nor is the presentation of ideas helped by Eliot's style of argument. The emphasis on disproving an assertion – which few of us would wish to make anyway – leaves the reader wondering what Eliot's own position is.

There is, however, the overall direction of these essays, and of Eliot's work more generally, that is more than relevant to today's debate. And not only the debate about welfare but, because of welfare's pervasive nature, the kind of society in which we live.

Eliot has a traditional framework into which he places his ideas. It is a view of the world and how it works. Central to this framework is Eliot's understanding of mankind, and his and her position in the universe.

That understanding is a Christian one. We are fallen creatures and yet ones who can be redeemed. Redemption does not automatically follow from our condition, but it is a possibility, and it is this hope which plays a central part in the Christian story.

That story begins in a garden and ends outside a city wall. The Old Testament recalls the Fall and the New Testament details the overcoming of death with the hope of resurrection. It is in Eliot's willingness to hold together these essential truths that his relevance to today's welfare debate is to be found.

It was this Christian view of the world which came under sustained attack during the Enlightenment. From a world where mankind was a fallen creature – to be redeemed in the next – redemption became a possibility in this world. In time redemption became more than a possibility. Man's perfectibility was to be worked by its own abilities.

That was not the end of the story, however. Man's perfectibility was not merely held as an ideal. It became a certainty. To stress the darker side of human nature was now to run the risk of being classified as an extremist, as a reactionary, as somebody on the Right, or even worse. It is at this stage of the debate that we see many of those purporting to be leaders of the Left losing touch with the real world.

Of course, this transformation took time to achieve. The disengagement from Christian beliefs in Britain has been a long and sorrowful process over many centuries. But it was only in the last century that those intellectuals who were active in mapping out this disengagement from belief expressed a concern about the transmitting and enforcing of moral values. Their hope was that Christian morality could be maintained without an adherence to Christian doctrine.

And, for so much of the last century or more, that has thankfully proved to be the case. Moreover, those on both Left and Right continued to hold a similar view on what constituted mankind. There were, of course, important differences of emphasis. On the Left there was greater optimism about the possibility of mankind's decency pulling civilisation in a more enlightened direction. On the Right a greater attention would be placed on what used to be termed man's sinful nature, his base desires and self-centredness. From this standpoint a note of danger was sounded to those who believed that the whole of the human race would readily conform to the lives of those who were the most altruistic and had the least personal ambition or least wish to exercise power.

Here I emphasise again that, generally speaking, while there were these differences dividing radicals and socialists on the one hand from conservatives on the other, the dominant characteristic was nevertheless a shared understanding of human character and the nature therefore of the putty which politicians had to use as the stuff of politics. And this common approach lasted for an uncommonly long period of time.

We have only to look at the contributions of trade unionists, in Parliament, in their own union, and in the running of the welfare state before 1945, as an illustration of the shared assumptions crossing the political divide. The struggle was for a better world, but there were few illusions about how this was to be gained, or of the qualities of the rank and file.

The superiority of one's beliefs was not to be confused with the superiority of the individual characters amassed on one's side. A cursory examination of trade union and friendly society rulebooks, and the list of rights and duties, of rewards and punishments, would quickly disabuse anyone of a contrary view.

In what Eliot saw as a Christian understanding of mankind lies considerable value for today's debate, both on how politics operates and, as part of that, the framework within which welfare functions.

The Gospel has two models of political activity. There is that of the light on the hill, the beams of which give out hope and direction to the travellers of this world. Here Christians are called to remain apart and to set out an ideal. Similarly, there is a political model in the analogy of the role of yeast in the baking of bread. And just as the yeast loses its identity in carrying out its function, to a large extent, so does the Christian activist who is involved in the day to day activities of politics.

The New Testament does not tell us which role — prophet or activist — is the most desired. The choice is left to the Christian citizen to make. Judgment is required in making this choice although, I guess, our make-up helps to direct us in one direction or the other. Some people have qualities which set them apart. Others are more gregarious and are natural team players and activists. Events also play some part in the choice of the type of Christian discipleship. George Bell found himself a prophet in speaking out against the saturation bombing of Germany in the last war. In contrast, others, like Basil Jellicoe, began changing housing policy, and the housing movement, as it is called in this country, by the activist role played in improving the housing conditions in their parish.

Whatever the role, Christian prophets and activists should be bound together by a shared view about human nature. The modern prophet will probably give greater stress to the role of hope in Christian teaching, while the activist is likely to be more aware of our fallen natures. But here again generalisations are rather crude tools by which to arrange what actually happens in practice. Many of the Old Testament prophets, for example, spelt out only too often where the darker side of our nature is leading us. And activists, like Jellicoe, were driven by the possibilities of an improved environment being reflected in better lives being lived.

Judgment and a sense of balance are required of Christians – and indeed of anyone else come to that – who wish to make a constructive contribution to politics. Balance is one of the most under-rated of political virtues. Here again the Church has something distinctive to say in the realm of how ideas impact on human events.

History teaches us that heresy does not usually come from the pedalling of some particular falsehood. Much more treacherously, heresy usually arises when one truth is taught in isolation from other truths. Here our natural guide against error is relaxed. The single truth can hold us mesmerised.

This holds for politics too. It is a truth to express the noble side of human nature. It is also an equal truth to remember our fallen nature. To express only our noble side is to give a false impression of what the vast majority of human beings are really like. It is a dangerous guide to action in the real world. But to dwell only on the darker side of our being is similarly a dangerous starting point for political action. What is required is to hold these two truths in balance.

That is true of all political activity (and most human activity too) and never more so than in respect of welfare. To see welfare in purely idealistic terms is only to take the debate back to where it was, for example, in the 1960s and 1970s. Here an unsustainable position was attempted. Individuals were driven only by altruism. Self-interest was banished to the very margins of welfare. Welfare claimants were all of the noblest quality. Fraud was therefore not so much an impossibility as an inconceivable act.

But the opposite case which began to be pushed in reaction to the unreality of the idealist was equally flawed. People do not only act on the most limited interpretations of self-interest. Nor are most claimants out to commit fraud.

Successful welfare needs to be built on holding together both of these two truths about human nature. To ignore the dark side is to court disaster as people quickly learn how to work the system to their advantage. But likewise, simply to forget how claimants can in certain circumstances look after their neighbour, in terms of the Good Samaritan, is to wipe out a crucial part of normal human behaviour.

The skill is to hold these two truths in some balance. What that balance is depends partly on the personalities concerned. It also depends on the circumstances in which individuals are called upon to operate. Eliot's stance, I guess, was in part a reflection of his own nature. But it may be that he was such an effective spokesman because his melancholic nature gave a particularly radical cutting edge against the unbalanced idealism which dominated politics in the wake of the Versailles Peace Treaty.

Eliot's melancholic approach would, I suggest, have been highly relevant in trying to rescue the welfare debate in the three decades from the 1960s onwards. Here Eliot would have understood why welfare had to work with, rather than against, the grain of human nature. He too would have seen the need to prevent a system ignoring the potential for fraud. Yet Christian hope would have led him to concede a role for idealism in the proper order of things.

Thinking the unthinkable about welfare was never the task of Government. It was a crucial activity, however, for Opposition. One part of that process was to rethink welfare around a Christian view of human nature, although no one, of course, expressed the task in such terms.

Part of thinking the unthinkable was to begin reconstructing welfare so it fitted with, rather than rubbed against, the grain of human nature. That, sadly, is not what is now happening. Eliot's voice would have been a powerful reminder to the Government that human nature can be ignored – but only for so long, before reform comes crashing around the ears of the reformers. It is here in this message that part of the enduring value of all Eliot's work, including *The Idea of a Christian Society*, is to be found.

Notes
★ An address given at Lambeth Palace Library on 17 May, 1999
1 This paper was one of four given to a symposium

organised by the St Gabriel's Trust on T. S. Eliot's *The Idea of a Christian Society* which was published by Faber in 1939. The symposium papers were published by the Trust in 1999 under the title *T. S. Eliot's The Idea of a Christian Society*.

6. Altruism, Self-Interest and the Sustainability of Welfare*

I present three themes which are linked together by the way their political implications interact. The first theme comes from an examination of expenditure patterns on welfare. Here I am not concerned with the crude total, although that is interesting in itself. It is upon the disproportionate growth in means-tested welfare within this total that I wish to concentrate. The second theme centres on the role altruism and self-interest play in the mind of voters. I suggest that while altruism plays a part in all human activity, and public welfare is no exception, the oxygen feeding this sentiment in the main comes from self-interest. In the last theme I argue that, while the exercise of altruism has a civilising and even graceful effect on civil society, it is too weak an impulse upon which to build a public system of welfare. Moreover, self-interest and altruism need to be held in balance, with self-interest being the dominant value. If this balance is overturned by altruism being given too prominent a role, the likelihood is of a political backlash which endangers the very operation of altruism itself within public welfare.

The means-tested welfare state

First, the growth of different welfare expenditures. For understandable reasons politicians and commentators spend a fair amount of effort measuring the size and gauging the growth of the social security budget. Understandably, I say, as the DSS budget currently consumes 1 in 3 pounds collected from taxpayers. But I do not believe this to be the most important question in this area. The official Opposition tries to pin the Government down on a pre-election pledge that it would cut the social security budget. The measurements in this debate are left a little vague. Is the objective to cut the budget in money terms, to cut its real growth, to cut its rate of increase, or to cut it as a proportion of the GDP?

The welfare reform Green Paper[1] was quite clear on this issue. Welfare expenditure would continue to grow. What else could be envisaged when, to take just one example, an ever greater proportion of the population is living beyond the normal retirement age and doing so for a few decades rather than for a few years? Pension expenditure has to rise if pensioner income is not to decline. What the Green Paper was clear upon, however, was that the taxpayers' share of this growing welfare bill should fall. In money terms state welfare might well continue to grow. The budget might even grow as a proportion of GDP. But other forms of welfare based upon a private and mutual contract would grow even faster.

While the global figures need to be monitored to ensure that this objective is being achieved, I would make a plea for politicians and commentators to cease concentrating on the crude overall size of the taxpayers' welfare bill – the stuff of what ought now to be yesterday's headlines. The task at hand is to focus attention on how radical is the changing composition of that bill.

To do so, let us step back in history and briefly consider how Beveridge saw the social security bill evolving after the implementation of his great report *Social Services and Allied Services*. His aim, as I am sure you will recall, was to abolish want by implementing a raft of national insurance benefits which would be paid at a high enough level to prevent individuals or families becoming poor as they lived through what is rather less than poetically described as the different stages of our life cycle. There would, of course, be a small number of people who, for special reasons, failed to build up the insurance contribution which would offer this contract. But their number, which might not be inconsiderable in the first instance, would decline in time as near universal insurance records were acquired.

That this vision had man-made flaws built into it from the very start need not detain us. The fall of the New Jerusalem has been recorded many times already for those interested in the history. But these flaws made a major difference to the budget, and this can be seen quite easily from the history of post-war welfare by turning to the social security budget for as Beveridge thought it would appear. Beveridge projected that the means-tested budget which accounted for 11 per cent of the welfare budget in 1945 would fall to just 5.5 per cent 20 years later.

Beveridge's 20-year projection was not far out. The 10 per cent of budget spent on means-tested benefits in 1950 remained constant for the next 20 years. Thereafter the trajectory was to change dramatically. Currently means-tests swallow about 35 per cent of the welfare cake.

Post-war welfare has been characterised not merely by a growing number of people eligible for a growing range of welfare benefits, but for these trends to be skewed in an ever more dominant means-tested direction. A scheme of reform which envisaged the near annihilation of means-testing had resulted in 1979 in one in every six households having at least one member drawing one of the many means-tested benefits then available.

Eighteen years later, at the close of the Tory administrations of Margaret Thatcher and John Major, this proportion had doubled – up to one in three of all households had at least one member drawing some form of means-tested support. And with that transformation in the composition of the welfare bill, I leave this aspect of the debate in order to introduce a second theme which I will then argue gains a particular importance once we bring back into focus the changing expenditure pattern of the modern welfare budget.

Competing motives

This second theme is the relationship between altruism and self-interest as sustaining forces in today's welfare. On many occasions I have put forward my belief that self-interest is the most powerful of the ever-present range of emotions which make up the human character. In the early days I made such an expression of belief unadorned by any modifying subordinate clauses. The aim was to shock the listener out of the malaise into which I believe the Centre Left's contribution to the debate had been so disastrously wooed.

Many people then saw the role ascribed to altruism in public policy as a crucial factor dividing Left and Right in politics. I did not believe that the then left-wing position that gave altruism either a total or a pre-eminent role in shaping welfare, either fitted known experience or, because of this, was sustainable in electoral terms.

To shift the course of political debate, particularly if such an action is being sought by a backbencher, usually requires a line to be stated with such clarity, and in such brevity, that the message can appear more than a little stark, not to say somewhat shocking to political activists who had been fed a contradictory diet over many decades. And certainly the importance I attach to self-interest in all human affairs – it does after all stem from our most basic survival instinct – was presented in as telling a form as possible.

I soon added another stage to my argument which centred on stressing that self-interest should be distinguished from selfishness, and that selfishness was itself a separate motive force from greed, and that it was important for sane debate to keep these distinctions in mind. Despite this, I believe that for a number of reasons the debate on the role of self-interest continued to be greeted with near disbelief.

This was the time when Mrs Thatcher was at the height of her powers, and it appeared that what I was saying was conceding far too much to this much-hated villain. Such hatred would have lain in wait for any politician ever anxious and eager to overthrow a political orthodoxy. But Mrs Thatcher had certain characteristics which made her a particularly attractive lightning conductor for such emotions. People saw, or rather wished to see, the reassertion of self-interest as a prime political motive force as a concession too far to the Thatcherite doctrine.

Having the ability to make the political weather, to recall that famous observation about Joe Chamberlain's impact in contemporary politics, is reserved for the few and not the many. Riding the political surf is about the only opening for most politicians anxious to contribute to the political debate. But surf riders have to be aware of the dangers of their particular craft. They have a duty to try and win enough supporters during their ride that the direction of the surf board can be turned their way before the waves finally reach the shore. The leader of the Labour Opposition was in my calculations the most important person to win over before the tide landed the activists onto the beach. Of course there are risks with any such endeavour. But the alternative to taking such risks was to stand idly by as the debate continued to exclude Labour from beginning to set its own agenda.

Re-evaluating self-interest's role was part of the thinking the unthinkable exercise, which itself was one conducted from the Opposition benches, and was part of a much wider strategy of attempting to make Labour once again electable. Self-interest was viewed as a crucial building block in reshaping welfare for the millennium. These building blocks were also required for a successful appeal to the electorate.

To assert the primacy of self interest is not to argue that there are not other interests or motivations operating at one and the same time. To assert one truth does not entail the denial of equally valid other truths. A look at the amount given each year to charity and voluntary effort quashes any idea that self-interest only operates in the absence of other motives. But getting Labour on to the starting blocks for electoral recovery did require an evaluation of self-interest's importance as being above all other motive forces.

This stance would have been seen as a statement of the blindly obvious to practically all the participants in welfare's journey during the last century, indeed for much of this. The growth of mutual aid, of co-operation, and the spread of self-help organisations, bodies which changed the face of Victorian society decidedly for the better, were all firmly rooted in this understanding of human nature. How could it have been otherwise in a Britain which was then composed either of active believers, or others who drew upon the intellectual capital built up from century upon century of belief in Christianity and a Christian understanding of mankind.

These activists and their allies alike appeared to have the ability to hold at once at least two truths without feeling any inconsistency, or being charged with muddled thinking, or worse, of double dealing. Those working men and women who changed their own lives, and many of the lives of their follow citizens, saw promoting self-interest as natural as night following day and perceived their noble journey as one which was simultaneously driven by strong altruistic motives. Altruism was part of the journey, the fruits of its exercise were everywhere to be seen, but it was held in check by the stern reign of self-interest. Moreover, while a society denied all altruism is much the cruder and harsher for its absence, one based solely on altruism is but a Utopian voyage set to meet the same rocky end that all such endeavours have so far encountered.

To say that Man is a fallen creature is not to conclude the story. It is to observe that while he is down, he is not out. Hope of redemption is ever present and this is an equally important part of the Christian message. Not surprisingly, therefore, the post-war welfare state was one clearly based on self-interest while holding out a helping hand to those who at any one time were dealt a series of difficult cards to play. There was some redistribution from rich to poor, but most redistribution was to the same group of people who at one time were paying contributions, while at another were drawing benefits. The feeling that everyone – or at least practically everyone – was in it together engendered a spirit of camaraderie which was as supportive of those whose luck was least, as it was effective in taking care of contributors raising families, facing unemployment, or sickness, or retirement and finally death. While few may have known the pound, shillings and pence of how their contributions broke down over the whole range of entitlements, many saw the operation as a contract which struck them as both sensible and fair. It is the breakdown of this feeling of a fair contract that lies at the centre of the political debate which has erupted over welfare during these last two decades or more.

Undermining altruism

You will have gathered that I am now into the third theme. The Beveridge welfare state, and much before it, centred around self-interest, while licensing a degree of altruism to shine throughout the whole operation. Indeed, self-interest and altruism were the warp and weave of that single garment. But it took self-interest to ensure the contributions were more or less willingly paid, and from these payments the warp was constituted. Without this warp, the weave of the welfare state would have held no shape and would have very quickly become an unholy mess.

Welfare's weave has always been the means-tested side of the operation where benefits are awarded, not on a basis of contributions paid, but simply on need. And the strain on the system stems directly from the changing ratio of welfare based on contributions paid or duties such as caring performed, to one divorced from this clear idea of contract.

Worse still, as the two forms of welfare slip out of kilter (there will always be both types in any welfare state imaginable under current conditions – the key question is the ratio of one to the other) there is a much predicted impact on the nature of welfare. And here we meet another part of the then Opposition task of thinking the unthinkable – that eventually it again became accepted thinking on most of the Centre Left that welfare was not a neutral agency, but was an active participant in shaping how people's actions, behaviour, and thereby character developed.

Here I want to stress another side to the debate on how means-tests impact by discouraging work, savings and honesty. It concerns how I believe the rapidly changing imbalance towards a means-tested welfare is impacting on the exercise of altruism throughout welfare. Let me explain. Despite the general refrain of how ever more individuals in the public arena conduct themselves in an ever less civilised manner, a view about what constitutes common decencies, and their importance to civilised life, still prevails. Altruism is both part of these common decencies and also protected and defended by their existence. But these common decencies, which until recently operated without public comment, are increasingly under attack. The sword cutting at their roots blandishes the title of unfairness.

A growing sense of unfairness surrounds the operation of welfare. The letters from pensioners who have responded to the clarion call of previous Governments to look after themselves, to buy their own homes, to save, and to seek jobs paying often only modest work's pensions, testify to a growing anger at being in a worse financial position than other pensioners who have simply failed to respond to the self-same appeal and now depend totally on means-tested support. And while you and I might rejoin that such pensioners probably had little opportunity to save, or buy their own home, these correspondents detail otherwise of neighbours who have always been in the habit of spending today, leaving taxpayers to pick up their bills tomorrow.

This sense of growing unfairness and, as a result, a declining support for the total welfare package, comes in large part from the observation that many taxpayers are themselves on very modest means, and yet are called upon to pay a growing means-tested bill which rewards citizens for behaving recklessly, improvidently, carelessly or, more simply, badly. Many, although by no means all, of these welfare recipients appear to mock the values of those still playing by the rules, who have been good citizens, and who are actively engaged in strengthening civil society. It is from this group of good citizens that the strongest cry has come for a more restrictive view of welfare, and particularly that part which is underpinned by altruism.

Altruism is being undermined by a falling degree of tolerance by taxpayers. It is being undermined too by the behaviour of a growing proportion of altruism's recipients who see welfare as being awarded to them unconditionally. Without the cover given by self-interest the operation of altruism in welfare comes increasingly under attack.

Conclusion

I have been arguing to three themes. I have again asserted my belief that self-interest is the most powerful, but far from the only, motive force in each of us. Altruism also plays its part. But a habitual danger of the centre-left is to have such a distorted view of human nature that altruism is given a role in the grand scheme of public affairs that it is simply unable to bear. The exercise of altruism is an important aspect of a civilised country, and it naturally has a place in public welfare. But that role not only cannot be maintained in isolation, but needs to be protected by self-interest. Get the two motive forces out of kilter, and altruism is the inevitable loser.

Such a position is fast approaching in public welfare. Throughout modern times, certainly since the middle of the last century, public welfare (which, of course, wasn't always synonymous with state welfare) was based on the idea of contract – contributions earned entitlements.

Any system of welfare worthy of its name has to cater for those who are, at any one time, unable to make the contract. In private welfare this aspect has been covered by charity and in public welfare by means-tested assistance. The means-tested side of welfare, awarded on the basis of need, not earned entitlement, was envisaged as a minor or emergency side of public welfare. Here, in this subsidiary role, altruism prospered.

That subsidiary role is being transformed. In 1979 one in six households were drawing means-tested welfare. Eighteen years later this proportion had doubled. Once means-tested welfare becomes a major player it affects behaviour. It teaches citizens not to save, not to work, and not to tell the truth. That is bad enough; but worse follows. Means-tested welfare is based on the principle that failure should be rewarded. Why keep up membership of the contract when a better deal can be gained by opting for means-tested welfare? And this trend becomes ever stronger as means-tested welfare spreads and a greater and greater proportion of the population learns that it cannot make itself much better off, if better off at all, other than by giving up, accepting failure, and simply joining the ranks of those who are unable fully to provide for themselves.

But while some give up and accept the rewards of failure, others are appalled by the unfairness that is created. It is this growing sense of unfairness which is leading to a backlash against that aspect of public welfare which is run on altruistic rather than on clear contractual lines. Far from self-interest and altruism being diametrically opposed motives, I have been arguing that only within a system reflecting self-interest can altruism safely survive in the long run. Altruism is now being asked to support too great a part of public welfare and this status quo cannot hold.

Appendix

The views expressed here, and the beliefs which underpin them, have come under attack most stridently from Tim Gorringe, the Professor of Theology at Exeter, as nothing more than 'a right-wing analysis dressed up as Christian theology' (Tim Gorringe, 'The Gospel according to Frank', *Christian Socialist*, Christmas, 1998). The attack is of interest primarily because it brings into the open what are different approaches to politics upon which I would like to comment. The Gorringe charge sheet is important because therein he sets out what he sees as a superior form of political activity, whether he realises it or not.

The charge sheet reads thus: I have made the fallen status of human nature my starting point and see self-interest as the great driving force in human affairs. This has led me to question those who see altruism as the main motivating force in welfare. I see successful Centre Left politics as providing a framework where natural decent instincts guided by self-interest are allowed to enhance the common good. To this interpretation Gorringe's views cannot be in doubt. Gorringe proclaims:

> Whatever we think of Field's policies what needs to be said loud and clear is that these assumptions about human nature have nothing to do with the Gospel ... it is one thing to argue with Bismarck, that you cannot run a state by the ethics of the Sermon on the Mount and claim that the voters of middle England understand human nature better than Jesus of Nazareth: politicians since Pontius Pilate have thought the same. What is

offensive is to have this right-wing analysis dressed up as Christian theology.

It is worth dwelling on a number of aspects of this statement. Take the rather surprising opening 'Whatever we think about Field's policies'; to most voters this is the central concern, but not so with Gorringe. More important is his belief that my views 'have nothing to do with the Gospel'. It is only in the sectarianism found on the political Left that such comments are made. The Right doesn't usually question the integrity of a person's belief; they attack the views. Ronald Preston reminds us of an extreme example of where such a sectarian approach can lead. In the 1930s, Reinhold Neibuhr's *Moral Man and Immoral Society* was offered to the SCM Press for publication in this country. The editor turned the work down on the grounds that he believed it to be unChristian.[2]

To Gorringe's charge that my views 'have nothing to do with the Gospel' I make the following observation. I do so as a politician; Gorringe is the theologian. Gorringe writes that lying behind much of what I have to say is a pre-Christian theology. I do not hold the strict division between Old and New Testament which appears to inform Gorringe's thinking. I see the New Testament as a fulfilment of the Old, and not a denial. The law and the prophets were of huge importance to Jesus. I believe the views of both the Old and New Testaments need to be held in some kind of balance. They provide us with a major map and compass to guide our action. The texts do not constitute a detailed instruction manual of what we should or should not do.

Apart from a clear emphasis on the first two great Commandments, Jesus's teaching method was one of putting the question back to the questioner and asking what they believed to be the right course of action.

In place of programmes, the New Testament describes two approaches to political activity. Neither of which is commended over the other. There is, first, the idealistic model of political activity – the light on the hill. As with the lighthouse, the quality of a person's life, and sometimes what they say, can shine out and act as a beacon, giving out both hope and direction.

There is also the active campaigning associated with the political activists which, in the New Testament, is given as the example of yeast in the making of bread. Instead of standing apart, acting as a beacon, the political activist is absorbed in the process of bringing about change.

The first approach, the light on the hill, suggests a life apart for the politician. The second ensures the loss of his or her identity while attempting in some small way to influence the great scheme of things. Some politicians switch between these roles, judging which, in particular circumstances, is likely to be most effective. Others, like Gandhi, manage to combine both roles simultaneously, but Gandhi was rather special. Both roles aim at influencing the debate and the conduct of affairs. Individuals have to choose which they believe the more effective, and both sides, not just one, have to answer for their judgment.

At another point Gorringe writes of a fundamental Christian perception which is embodied in the welfare state. Gorringe remarks:

ALTRUISM, SELF-INTEREST AND THE SUSTAINABILITY OF WELFARE

Duncan Forrester expresses in *The Future of Welfare*: 'Worth is attributed by God to human beings independent of achievement; it is not something to be earned. Human beings are ... beloved by God ... apart from achievement ... or even stakeholding. Christian character is gracious, generous, loving and just. And a decent society must do something to incorporate such values into its welfare provision. Forrester is talking about grace, the radical giftedness which is at the heart of Christian perceptions of the human in a way which autonomy, independence and, God help us, self-interest, simply are not. He demands that that be taken on board as a political, and not just as a theological, reality.

But what does 'taking on board' mean? I ask the question because it illustrates another aspect of political activity. Political activity for me is all about being successful in the sense of trying to influence events. I hope you will not misunderstand what I am trying to say. Views are not propounded simply to be successful. But aiming for success is crucial. Making a statement or 'taking on board' are preludes to a whole range of activities which will finally see those views operating within the wider society. To view 'taking on board' as the end game is to reduce political activity to mere gesturing. It may of course be that times are such that few pay much attention to the views being expounded. That stance is adapted not simply for personal gratification, but to have some impact, however long-term that may be. Both the lighthouse and the yeast analogy are about making a difference. Which model is adopted depends partly on the time and the circumstances and partly on the gifts of the political activist as well as how circumstances and talents interact.

I do not wish to deny, nor have I ever denied, the importance of the views contained in the quotation from Duncan Forrester. I do not turn my back on the views I built up working for 10 years with CPAG in the LPU. Nor do I deny what I have learnt for 20 years representing an inner-city seat. Forrester neatly puts into the welfare debate proper stress on Christian hope – what can be achieved over and above what might rationally be thought possible. The question which obsesses my thinking is how the exercise of 'taking on board' can be translated into legislation which will work and be sustainable. It is on this point that a sentimental view of human nature which underplays or even ignores sin, both original and actual, leaves such proponents of change looking distinctly unworldly, to put it politely. The price the unworldly pay is usually to be excluded from political power. There is nothing inherently wrong with such a result. It may be a person's vocation to adopt it. It might even be thought that it will in the longer term help reshape the practical political agenda. What appears Utopian to one generation can become bread and butter politics to another. But it is a fallacy to argue that just because some Utopian views move from the world of dreams into the realm of practical politics, all must do so. And this is never more so than for those denying the facts of human nature governing how we operate as human beings.

One judgment politicians of the Gorringe school have to make – for politicians they are when they actively involve themselves as Christian Socialists in the political process, and judgments they have to make, whether they consciously realise it or not – is the price the poor have to pay for the adoption of either of the strategies touched upon here in this paper. We have long ceased to inhabit a world where the interests of the working class and the poor are identical. With this divergence the poor, who are a distinct minority of voters, are ever more dependent upon the effectiveness of politicians espousing their cause in the political process. It is, I maintain, the poor who pay the greatest price if the Centre Left fails to adopt a strategy which, while commanding majority support, also protects their interest. Moreover, I maintain, if the Centre Left is captured by the ranks of the unworldly, to whom voters are even less likely to entrust political power, the poor are clearly the biggest losers. No amount of 'taking on board' this or that stance can hide the hard facts that the poor by themselves are no longer the movers and shakers in the political process in this country. The Centre Left can now win without the votes of the poor. What I have been attempting to do for most of my political career is to try and devise strategies which, while furthering the interests of the majority, are ones which also protect and enhance the interests of the poor.

Notes
* A paper delivered at Sarum College in Salisbury on 25 September, 1999.
1   A New Contract for Welfare, New Ambitions for Our Country, Cm 3805.
2   Ronald Preston, *Crucible*, Special Reviews Issue, Summer 1999, p. 276.

7. The Role of Welfare in an Inclusive Society*

Inclusive welfare is bound up with the idea of universal provision. The stress should be placed on the universal, for not only does it ensure inclusiveness, but it underscores a key Labour value. It symbolises the basic equality which we as a movement believe should be accorded to each and every individual.

The debate needs to centre on the circumstances in which universal provision is essential, and how best can this goal of universal provision be achieved.

Despite rising income – up threefold this century – the majority of us become poor very quickly if we lose the ability to work (and sometimes we are poor in work). Universal provision needs to underpin our standard of living when we cannot work, and such provision needs to be offered without a test of income. Welfare must act as a springboard to further self-advance, and not a ceiling curtailing honest endeavour, as is so often the result with the means-tested approach.

Because of my belief in a basic equality of respect which should be accorded to each of us, and because part of thinking the unthinkable was the acceptance that welfare affects behaviour, I have always argued the case for universal provision for the minimum income guarantees in welfare. Where

I have failed in this debate is to convince a large enough part of the Labour movement (as opposed to the electorate) that the primary objective of universal provision cannot now be advanced by the old-fashioned menu of state socialism.

Such an approach was probably inevitable after the Second World War. It no longer appears as an attractive proposition to a growing proportion of voters.

For those now committed to universal provision I believe we must keep a clear distinction between the ends – universal provision and why we subscribe to this – and the means of achieving this end. The means to that end now has to become a genuine partnership between collective – i.e. Government-run and mutually owned schemes – and the private sector. The failure to win this argument of the Labour movement distinguishing between means and ends has left the objective – universal provision – open to easy attack, and has freed the Government to advance its selective, means-tested strategy.

Advocating a new programme for universalism relates to the debate over our core voters. Labour cannot now win simply by relying on its core voters. The Prime Minister won the last time (and it was very much his victory) by reaching voters not usually touched by the Party's traditional appeal. Indeed, I believe we can win next time by ignoring our core voters. That *doesn't* mean we should. It puts a moral duty on the leadership not to forget the groups the advancement of whose interest was the reason why Labour came into existence. But it also puts a similar duty on the active membership. We have a duty, with the leadership, to advance programmes which simultaneously meet the needs of poorer people and those who are thankfully more affluent.

How can this be done? I give one example by describing the kind of stakeholder pension scheme I argued for in Government.

Any fool can devise pension schemes for the rich, and many have. The crunch issue is how do we advance a pension reform which includes the poor.

I believe this can be achieved by making stakeholder pensions a guarantee. The guarantee will be set at a level of average earnings when an individual retires after paying full contributions. The guarantee will be made up from the national insurance retirement pension and a new, growing, funded element.

This guarantee lifts everybody free of means-tested assistance. Every contributor therefore knows that if they are able to save in addition to their pension contributions they will keep every extra penny of savings. At the current time most ordinary people cannot now save enough to lift themselves above the Government's means-tested minimum income guarantee. The Government's stakeholder proposals cannot succeed for they have been holed below the water line by this minimum earnings guarantee.

Because this stakeholder guarantee cannot be bought in the private market it has appeal to people on higher income who will view it as the first tier of their retirement income. Because of this appeal it will be possible to have graduated contributions for the flat-rate guarantee. Graduated contributions provide money for the poor who cannot afford to pay or who engage in socially desirable tasks such as caring for children or elderly relatives, i.e. who behave as decent citizens.

How the funded side of the stakeholder pension is to be organised should be an issue of debate. But the scheme has to be compulsory and needs to be introduced at a set starting date so that everyone who turns 20 years old, for example, is brought within the scheme. In the following year the next wave of 20-year olds will be brought within the scheme.

Closing the supply routes to poverty in old age opens up a new debate on how we should help existing pensioners and those future pensioners who will be poor before the new stakeholder scheme comes fully into existence. Governments can in these circumstances be generous with taxpayers' money as they know that there is a time limit to any new pension expenditure.

A further advantage of a universal compulsory stakeholder scheme is that it allows other reforms in the welfare state to be conducted without damaging existing contributors. For example, the universal stakeholder pension allows very cheap life cover as everybody who reaches a certain age comes within the scheme. In those circumstances it is right and proper to close national insurance widow's benefits to those who will be covered by the new life insurance carried on the back of the stakeholder proposals. Having everybody in the stakeholder scheme allows the life cover to be acquired at the lowest possible rates.

Notes
* A paper given to the Tribune Conference: Democratic Socialism in the 21st Century on 17 July, 1999.

8. Welfare: A Bird's Eye View*

Histories of the welfare state usually begin around 1945. The 1940–50 period does mark a particular point in the history of welfare in Britain. But to begin the story here distorts the record. It promotes the idea of welfare developments in this country as part of a collective train journey which began with Lloyd George and ended with Mr Attlee, Labour's 1945 Prime Minister, safely steering the train into a collective welfare state terminal.

The mixed economy of welfare
The theme of most welfare histories is 'the coming of the welfare state' as though all previous forms of welfare were temporary and incomplete, that it was inevitable Britain's welfare should be ultimately dominated by state provision, and that, somehow, the journey is now at an end. However, if we step back only 100 years – and use this as a vantage point to look forward – we have a very different perspective. In the 19th century Britain's welfare was characterised by voluntary provision, with mutual and friendly societies delivering a whole range of benefits. Local authorities and voluntarily run hospitals, together with a national system of panel doctors, were financed from health insurance contributions, which were set by the state and collected through

mutually owned societies.

If we move back further still we gain yet another perspective of how welfare was delivered collectively, free of the state. In mediaeval times many hospitals were church-run, though the word hospital should not be understood in today's terms. Back then such places were communities where the elderly and frail in particular were looked after.

Parishes, the first basic administrative units in Britain, also had a responsibility to their poor. The Elizabethan Poor Law enshrined this right with the practice of sturdy and less sturdy beggars being sent back to their parish of origin ostensibly for help. This system, although modified, remained largely intact until the offensive launched by the Utilitarian reformers. For them, no fiddling with the facts was beyond the pale if it could discredit the old regime. The new Poor Law of 1834 was the result of this campaign, and where the principle of 'less eligibility' was enforced – help in the new system would only be offered if a person came into the 'House', as the poor law institution was known – a standard of living awaited them which was below that on which the poorest labourer could survive.

Never-ending reform
No system of welfare, then or now, remains set for any great length of time. The new Poor Law was never completely enforced. Poor Law guardians, whose job it was to administer the new scheme, all too often ran the system on the cheap by building only a single house, thereby failing to provide for the able-bodied workman on the one hand, and the frail and ill on the other. Others, thankfully, stood up to

central authority and provided relief outside the workhouse, hence its name 'outdoor relief'. Indeed this form of relief for the aged poor was so common that reformers regrouped themselves in the last decades of the 19th century to attack what most citizens saw as a pay-as-you-go pension scheme, i.e. they paid the poor rate when they could work to support others, and drew a pension from the parish when they were old. In principle this system is very similar to today's state pension, and serves to emphasise how frequently old welfare wine is politically marketed in new bottles.

The 19th century reformers' zeal came under attack from four other sources. First, the Poor Law advocates fell foul of their own propaganda. It was believed that, as people became poor largely because of perceived moral failings, a rigorously enforced Poor Law would serve to improve behaviour and lower bills. On this score the Poor Law enthusiasts began to dig a huge hole into which they were eventually pushed. Britain's prosperity increased but so too did Poor Law costs.

Next, for most of the 19th century working people, fully believing in self-help but also in mutual aid, built up their own welfare state through mutual aid bodies and friendly societies. So successful were these self-governing organisations, operating as little democracies, that their existence helped clinch the vote for an ever-increasing number of working people. In time, these new voters became interested in what politicians were offering in the way of welfare reform.

Third, views on poverty changed, and changed radically. At the time of the Poor Law Amendment Act in 1834, the debate was about how best to deal with pauperism. By the end of the century much more attention was being paid to the causes of poverty. Unemployment, for example, entered the language for the first time in the 1880s.

This too was the age of the first social survey and the results heightened public awareness of the extent of poverty. Charles Booth, the shipping magnate, spent a very large part of his fortune surveying the poor. One of his results showed that most people never came within the ambit of the Poor Law until they were too old and frail to work. This led Booth to support the introduction of state pensions.

Fourth, trade unions began striking bargains with their employers so as to regularise the size of their members' wage packets. Deals were done over hours worked and the length of working weeks during time when trade was bad in order to prevent working people from losing the whole of their income. Employers began company welfare schemes, often, but not invariably, as a means of countering growing trade union power. Contributory pensions were set up partly in the belief that workers contributing to their company pension would be less militant as they had a stake in their firm's prosperity. Sickness and health schemes also arose in order to ensure as fit a labour force as possible. The early years of this century witnessed a massive advance in trade union numbers, and this growth was paralleled in the forward march of company welfare schemes.

Advent of state welfare

Lloyd George did not therefore invent the welfare state. As we have seen, it was already very much in existence. But he did, along with a young Winston Churchill, refine the concept and drive it forward into the arms of the state – surprising for a Liberal politician. But we have jumped too far ahead in our story.

The 1906 landslide victory of the Liberal Government was not based on a programme of welfare reform. Indeed, it did its best not to discuss it. But reform came. In order to protect the friendly societies – many of whom were facing financial difficulties with members in effect drawing sick pay as though it was a retirement benefit – a non-contributory, means-tested old-age pension was introduced for those of 70 or more. At the time average life expectancy for men was 48 years!

National health and a more limited coverage, unemployment insurance, were introduced by the 1911 Act. Contribution and benefit levels were laid down by Parliament, but friendly societies and mutually-owned bodies operated the health scheme.

The insurance principle was advanced to finance this new welfare because the Liberal Government was anxious not to raise income tax and alienate the bedrock of its support. It therefore followed Bismarck's lead. In Germany Bismarck had faced even greater barriers to tax-based welfare. The German Chancellor did not then have the power to levy taxes on income. The insurance principle, now regarded as a crucial aspect of state welfare, originally met with considerable hostility. Lloyd George won over the initial opposition with his tripartite financing from worker, employer and taxpayer. Hence his cry to the workers of '7d for 3d'.

Neville Chamberlain added to this insurance base with the Widows', Orphans and Old Age Contibutory Pensions

Act of 1925. Pensions were paid from 65 and a widow's benefit was introduced. But these inter-war years were dominated by unemployment. And it was the financial chaos resulting from botched attempts to provide income for the mass unemployed, while maintaining an insurance fund, which helped reposition trade unionists, and others, on the question of state or voluntary-based welfare. The use of a household-based means-test for unemployment assistance added grist to the mill for this campaign.

Enter Beveridge

An enquiry was established in 1941 to propose how best to tidy up state welfare. Beveridge seized the opportunity, rewrote the script, and then redesigned the contours of British welfare. The publication of his report was fortuitously delayed. When it was produced in November 1942 it followed hard on the heels of the Allies' first major victory of the Second World War. Implementing Beveridge was immediately seen as part of winning the peace.

The prize was security 'from the cradle to the grave'. Although largely a synthesis of ideas (including Beveridge's) which had been around for some time, it was the blueprint for conquering want, one of the five giants Beveridge declared should be slain by way of post-war reconstruction. Each giant was countered by:

- The 1944 Butler Act which reformed schooling.
- The 1944 commitment to full employment.
- The Family Allowance Act of 1945.
- The 1946 National Insurance Act.

- The 1948 National Health Act, aimed at achieving that very objective, and established for the first time a national minimum.

But, as always, the world did not stand still. Although for sometime in the 1950s and 1960s welfare provision did just that. How to finance the NHS increasingly became a key political issue. Insurance benefits were not paid at a high enough level to prevent many pensioners from becoming poor, and by the 1970s full employment began taking a battering which it has had to endure until recently. The political caravan had once again moved off in search of new ideas.

Thatcherism

There was never a coherent Thatcherite approach to welfare. Following the main haemorrhage of manufacturing jobs in the 1981–82 recession (exacerbated by the inept handling of the exchange rate), the formal abandonment of a full employment goal looked like a mere precaution against future political failure. The NHS budget continued to increase, driven upwards by a growing demand set by a combination of rising expectations, by health consumption becoming a lifestyle-type choice, by advances in medical technology, and by a rapid growth in life expectancy.

Welfare bills were confronted in two ways. Insurance benefits were hacked back with an ever-growing number of individuals pushed on to means-tested support rising from one in six of the population in 1979, to one in three in 1997. But the biggest savings for taxpayers (paid for by less generous pensions) came in 1980 with the switch to increasing the state retirement pension only in line with prices, and not by earnings if these were rising faster – as they invariably did.

By 1979 occupational pensions had grown from the modest initiatives recalled earlier into the great welfare success of this country. Alongside these pensions the Tories planted individually owned schemes, known as personal pensions. The advent of these schemes was their major welfare innovation. This advance, however, has been hampered by miss-selling – i.e. persuading people to leave occupational schemes to join a personal pension scheme which invariably entailed the loss of the employers' contribution, together with the imposition of very high charges – a double whammy if ever there was one. Even so Britain had more assets owned by occupational and personal pension schemes than the whole of the asset portfolio owned by the other European Community schemes combined.

And yet welfare bills continued to escalate in an apparently unstoppable fashion. Welfare was about to undergo another major rethink.

Welfare and character

When welfare was run by friendly societies and mutually owned organisations few questioned the fact that welfare affected how people behaved. Welfare was not simply strictly policed; the range of benefits fully recognised the danger that some people would claim benefit to which they were not entitled if the regime was slack. Welfare was seen not merely as a means of meeting a need, but by its organisation and the means of its delivery, it was conceived as a tool for building good character.

The biblical view of human nature — its fallen status, yet conceived to be redeemed — was lost sight of in left-wing intellectual circles by the 1960s. Welfare was seen primarily as an act of altruism and this paternalistic view was advanced behind the cover of politically correct statements, so much so that even the Right lost the confidence to express, let alone act on, the broader, age-old understanding of mankind.

The resulting paralysis of both will and mind resulted in little concern for how different types of welfare (insurance or means-tested) affected behaviour; and to raise the question of fraud was to be automatically deemed politically unbalanced.

'Thinking the unthinkable' was the task for Labour's final years in Opposition before 1997, and was part of the strategy of making Labour electable. It was never meant to be an activity undertaken in Government.

Thinking the unthinkable in Opposition took place across five inter-related areas.

- It was not simply a question of the size and the rate of growth of social security expenditure. The key issue was the growth of means-tested welfare and in particular how this form of provision affected the actions of recipients.
- Welfare was not therefore seen as a neutral agency operating in society. Rather it was one, which, for good or ill, helped determine motivation, shape action and thereby determine character.
- Welfare had to work with the grain of human nature.

Self-interest, one of the most powerful of human instincts, had to be the cornerstone around which welfare reform was built.
- A clear distinction had to be maintained between the means and the ends of welfare policy. In order to gain adequate universal pension coverage for instance, new partnerships between the private and mutual sector were necessary.
- Welfare reforms were not merely an add-on to the Government's constitutional reform programme. Proposals for building up membership organisations which are separate from the Government on the one hand, and privately owned companies on the other, would have a central role in rebuilding civil society, which itself was an aim of welfare reform.

A health warning

The present Government has now embarked on its programme of welfare reform. Time will tell how well it succeeds in implementing the unthinkable. Making reform workable is a more important objective. As I resigned as Welfare Reform Minister I will inevitably be seen as a biased observer. And bias in the welfare debate is something about which readers should continually be on their guard.

One notable academic observed that to study welfare was to highlight the values of the society within which that welfare was provided. I would argue that our values determine to a large extent what we observe. Hence it was observers believing in state collectivist solutions who have generally written up the story of the coming of the welfare state and the final arrival of state provision. Any deviation from this model is seen not just as defeat, but as essentially retrogressive. That view is now under attack.

As one of those who first questioned the inevitability, let alone the desirability, of state provision being welfare's final resting place, and who seeks to present welfare developments as a continuous story, I am open to the charge by those who believe in the correctness of state welfare solutions, of being equally biased.

Notes

* A paper prepared for the BBC Website, www.bbc.co.uk/education/history/writers/field1.shtml – *The Welfare State – Never Ending Reform*, August 1999.

9. It's The Economy, Stupid!*

Charles Murray believes the ready availability of welfare corrupts the populace and accounts for the inevitable surge in the numbers on benefit. Lawrence Mead believes that some families have now become so dysfunctional that they are not only unwilling but also unable to work without being compelled to do so.[1] He doesn't explain why such a state of affairs exists. I contend that the sharp shrinkage of the job market for semi-skilled and unskilled workers has been the catalyst for the rising welfare rolls and that once on the rolls for what appears like an indefinite period there are changes in attitude and behaviour for a significant number of poor people of working age.[2] It is also the loss of employability which has lessened young low-skilled males' attractiveness as spouses, and the loss of unskilled jobs for females in inner city areas, which has made single parenthood appear the best of a very limited range of options. While benefit conditionality for male claimants in Britain has a part to play in helping people back to work, this approach needs to be accompanied by demand-side policies if it is to be successful in the inner-city where benefit dependency, for obvious reasons, is most pronounced.

Unemployment and the welfare rolls

Lawrence Mead makes his contribution to the debate in his customarily attractive manner. He distances himself from those conservatives who view the decline in family norms as a consequence of the temptations presented by social security. He writes 'To directly strengthen the family may be beyond the reach of Government', but he quickly cheers himself up, and no doubt his readers, by adding shortly afterwards: 'If there is any way for Government to strengthen the family in America, it will probably emerge from current efforts to enforce work among welfare recipients'. Reforms based on enticing the poor to work have had little success. Hence America 'has lately taken more direct steps to move the poor into jobs'.[3]

I wish to argue also for the development of a more proactive welfare whereby such payments are made much more conditional on seeking jobs.[4] The composition of the welfare rolls in Britain is radically different from America. The British rolls are not dominated by single parent claimants to the degree they are in the States. It has been the collapse of manufacturing employment which has transformed the composition of Britain's welfare rolls. Welfare changed from being primarily concerned with retired claimants, to a system dealing with people of working age. It has been the collapse of the job market for semi-skilled and unskilled males which has had the greatest impact, both directly and indirectly, on both the composition of those on welfare and the length of time spent on welfare, and thereby on the functioning of families.

In the early post-war period the welfare rolls were composed largely of claimants who were retired.[5] This dominance of pensioners was such that their numbers rarely fell below 70 per cent of claimants. This position held right up to 1970, and even then pensioner's dependants remained in a clear majority until 1980. The fall in the proportion of pensioners was not brought about by fewer pensioners claiming. The opposite has occurred, with numbers of pensioners on welfare rising almost threefold. It was, rather, the impact of two major recessions in Britain which revolutionised the composition of the welfare rolls. The first of the two major post-war recessions, starting in 1980, saw the number of unemployed on welfare rise from less than 20 per cent of the total to over 40 per cent in the space of three years. By 1983, for the first time ever during the post-war period, there were more unemployed claiming benefit than there were pensioner claimants. That position was further reinforced by the recession that began in the early 1990s.

The severity of these recessions is seen in the data on the numbers in work in Great Britain. The size of the labour force rose in most years in post-war Britain. When earlier post-war recessions occurred, the fall in employment rarely amounted to more than half a million, or 1 in 50 of the total number of jobs. Moreover, a complete recovery was recorded within the space of two or three years. The recessions of the early 1980s and 1990s were of a quite different order. Within three years after 1980 1.5 million jobs were lost. Almost 2 million jobs were lost in the recession beginning in 1990 and the total number of jobs still had not reached the 1990 level 8 years later.

Loss of male jobs

These two recessions have had a lasting impact on the employment levels of male workers. While the total number of jobs in the economy has risen overall by a little over 2 million since 1979, the number of male jobs has fallen over the same period by half a million. While the number of women in work has risen by 2.5 million, this growth in the female labour force has not been uniform throughout the country. In some inner-city areas the number of women workers has fallen, although by far less than the dramatic collapse in the number of males in work in the same areas. The loss of male jobs has been particularly noticeable in the trades offering semi-skilled and unskilled workers job opportunities.

The constituency of Birkenhead which I represent in Parliament illustrates how growing national prosperity accompanied by a buoyant national labour market conceals considerable job deficits in some local labour markets. That Birkenhead is typical of inner-city areas in Britain can be seen from a recent study by the Joseph Rowntree Foundation.[6] In 1979 there were 20,900 men working full-time in Birkenhead, as well as 2,400 males in part-time employment. By 1997 the number of men in full-time work had dropped to 12,500 and the number of male part-time workers had also fallen, to 2,100. In case anyone sees these data as supporting the Murray thesis – welfare availability tempting people onto benefit – these years were marked by the closure of much of the heavy manufacturing base in Birkenhead including the shipyard and the steelmill. The number of women in full-time work in the constituency stood at 7,700 in June 1978 rising to 11,300 three years later. By September 1997 the number of women in full-time work had fallen to 8,800. Similarly the number in part-time work in the constituency, which had stood at 12,300 in 1978, had fallen 20 years later to 9,100.

I therefore disagree with what one commentator has billed as Mead's 'most striking argument', namely, that the availability of jobs is not a technical issue to be resolved by examining the appropriate data. Jobs are there, but the long-term workless poor, while 'dutiful', are 'defeated'.[7] Proactive welfare is relevant for the whole country, for even in those areas registering a major jobs deficit, some jobs still become available. But proactive welfare by itself is not adequate in those areas where the job cull has been massive. Here workers have every reason to feel defeated.

Impact on behaviour
In the years following the 1980 recession economists began talking of hysteresis. By this they meant that the recession had been so severe, and had so enfeebled some local economies, that the market could not engender its own recovery. But the severity of the recession not only affected how the local economy worked. It also had a similarly devastating impact on the behaviour of many people. It was the recession which pushed people onto the welfare rolls, and thereby changed the behaviour of some claimants. It was not that such behavioural changes resulted in welfare claims.

How was behaviour affected? Hysteresis on individuals and families resulted in the breakdown for many of the habit of work. It's as simple as that. The norm in the town where young males smartly moved from school into work was destroyed. Worklessness becomes the norm in some tightly defined areas. The hopelessness of being part of a huge stagnant pool of unemployed can defeat all but the most determined of individuals. And this hopelessness was not assuaged by drugs. The marital status of males was damaged. How can you start to plan a life together when all that is brought financially to the contract is a meagre welfare cheque? So marriage became an endangered species in the poorest areas. A new norm was quickly established. In one of the poorest parishes in Birkenhead a yearly total of 170 or so funerals was matched by as few as 3 marriages. It was not only young workers who were affected, although as a group they bore the brunt of the jobs collapse.[6] Older redundant male workers faced similar difficulties in finding a job in a far tighter labour market. But successive Tory Governments, wishing to see the unemployment count fall as elections approached, were active in persuading employment staff to transfer claimants to Incapacity Benefit, as it is now called, or at least to register them as sick.

The collapse in the job market also impacted on the numbers of young single parents. Why marry a fellow – supposing an offer is there – when a benefit claim as a single parent results in proportionately more money than marrying, particularly if the boyfriend also claims his welfare cheque, together with housing benefit, and sub-lets his flat while living with his girlfriend? More money to be sure, but hardly a more stable environment for children to grow up in. Here is just one example of benefit rules affecting behaviour once people are on the rolls. But it wasn't simply the collapse of suitable jobs for men with few skills which led to fewer men being able to fulfil their financial responsibilities as fathers. The self-same changes to the local labour market operated against women as well. Over a 20-year period the number of full-time and part-time jobs for women workers in Birkenhead fell by 2,500 and 2,200 respectively. Fewer full-time job opportunities now exist for young women before marriage, and there are also fewer part-time job opportunities for mothers to combine with family responsibilities should a marriage have taken place. And news on this front travels fast along the grapevine from older sisters and friends finding difficulty in supplementing their family income with part-time work. Faced with greater difficulty in getting a full-time job, and with far fewer young men able to accept the financial responsibility of fatherhood, some young women opt rationally for lone parenthood, usually, but not invariably, soon after they have left school.[8]

The Case for proactive welfare

To explain that the main cause of welfare's transformation lies in the economy is not to argue for welfare's status quo. A welfare operation designed to look after pensioners is clearly unsuitable once that operation is geared to a very large majority of claimants of working age. Hence the move in Great Britain to make welfare proactive. New Deal, introduced in Great Britain in 1998, is the most far-reaching of the welfare changes introduced so far by the Blair Government. All unemployed claimants without family responsibilities who are below the age of 25 and have been unemployed for 10 months have to accept one of a range of full-time options, including subsidised work, or lose benefit. This scheme is being extended to other claimants without family responsibilities.

The case for national proactive welfare schemes is twofold. The first is that, as has been already noted, the delivery of welfare was originally geared almost exclusively towards pensioners and these are no longer the majority of claimants. No-one seeking to set up welfare in Britain today would design the system that was put in place in the early post-war years which were characterised by full employment. With a tighter job market, and fewer jobs for life, an active employment service helping claimants into work is required. But secondly, such a service was also necessary to counter the feelings among groups of claimants that looking for work is hopeless, or is not an attractive enough proposition. That was a view which took root after the first major recession, and was reinforced by the second. While proactive welfare is most relevant in areas registering high employment, it also has a role in areas still characterised by high unemployment. Let me cite the example of Birkenhead again. Despite the size of the job deficit, jobs do become available, even at the peak of recession. The Wirral Employment Service, which covers Birkenhead and the surrounding area, helped 15,105 people into work in 1995–96 at a time when the local labour market was still fragile following a severe recession.

Proactive welfare, by concerning itself with the skill levels and attitudes of claimants, can play a part in improving the quality of labour on offer; and the availability of such labour may itself help stimulate job creation by employers who might not otherwise consider such a development. But while it is crucial to develop still further this 'help and hassle' strategy which underpins proactive welfare, this approach alone will not see significant reductions in unemployment in those areas suffering a major job deficit. In areas of persistently high unemployment, New Deal Mark 2 will need to consider much more direct means of influencing the demand for labour, as well as keeping a continual interest on the supply side issues.

Single parents

New Deal in Britain extends to single parents on benefit. The New Deal for Lone Parents targets single parents who have been on Income Support for more than eight weeks, and whose youngest child is in full-time schooling, with a package of job search, training and after-school care to help them into work. But the crucial difference between this part of the New Deal and those applying to all other able-bodied workers, is that the scheme is voluntary. Lone parents are invited to the employment office for an interview, but there is no sanction on those who refuse this invitation, let alone anything more demanding. This part of the New Deal was implemented nationally at the end of October 1998. By the end of June 1999 72,190 lone parents had attended an interview; of these 6,450 had left the scheme and found jobs.[9] The scheme is based on self-selection, and while some single parents have been helped into work, the likelihood is that many of these would have made that transition anyway.[10]

An assumption behind the view of many of those advocating more conditional welfare for single mothers in this country, as well as those blazing the trail in America, is that single mothers working leads to better functioning families. That may be so for single mothers with older children. In Britain single mothers have a right to draw benefit until their youngest child has reached 16. At some stage this rule will be reviewed. While policies helping those single mothers with younger children move into work when they wish to do so commands considerable, but not universal, support in this country, an approach which made the drawing of benefit conditional on seeking work, either after two years on benefit, or once children began school, would not win the support of the House of Commons, and I guess would be strongly opposed by a majority of voters.

Given this electoral bulwark against change, it is a pity the Government hasn't experimented more on ways of encouraging single parents back to work. It has so far cost £5,611 for each single parent moving back into work on the New Deal. Wouldn't it have been a worthwhile pilot to offer in one or two local areas, say, £2,000 to those single parents able to get back to work for at least a year? Here again is a difference with Mead. Some incentives are important in stimulating good behaviour. The Government's obsession with whether the poor's marginal tax rate is 70 per cent instead of 90 per cent is relevant on grounds of fairness, but not in making an effective contribution in moving people back to work.

It is through a policy of trying to raise skills of pupils in schools, of continuing that process for people once successfully placed in work, or seeking work, together with the development of proactive welfare policies to support people seeking work, that Government policy may help engender conditions conducive to stable families in areas of greatest poverty. But the hysteresis effect on people's behaviour following two major post-war recessions, and the changing views of what constitutes normal behaviour, is most clearly seen in inner-city areas where a cumulative process of disintegration appears to be at work. This should caution against claiming too much for what Government policy may achieve. Destruction is far, far easier than reconstruction. Stable families require an economy producing family wages and a surrounding culture which recognises and encourages the concept.

Conclusion

That Britain, like America, is reforming much of its welfare so that payments are conditional on actively seeking work, should not disguise the significant differences between the two countries. Welfare in America is primarily concerned with payments for single mothers. This is not the case in Britain, where unemployed males and disabled workers are also major welfare beneficiaries. But these differences should not detract from a common concern about the number of children being raised in fluid single-parent families.[12] Lawrence Mead sees the shoehorning of welfare claimants into work as possibly providing the most effective way of strengthening US families. I have argued that it has been the collapse of unskilled jobs, concentrated as these losses have been in inner-city areas, which has intensified the impact on society of changing views about marriage. The perceived near-irrelevance of marriage for many poorer people has been reinforced by tax and welfare systems giving privileges to single-parent status. Getting claimants in inner-city areas back to work is highly desirable on its own grounds, and will only be achieved by operating on both the demand as well as the supply sides of labour. But, as Lawrence Mead himself observes: 'To directly strengthen the family may be beyond the reach of Government', at least for Governments understandably concerned only with the short-term, and where the wish to find that ever elusive panacea is as strong as ever.

Notes
* A paper contributed to *Family Matters*, Australian Institute of Family Studies, Spring/Summer 1999.
1 See Lawrence Mead's essay in the same publication.
2 This is not to argue that the existence of welfare doesn't impact on behaviour and thereby the character of claimants, see my *Making Welfare Work*, ICS, 1995, and *How to Pay for the Future*, ICS, 1996.
3 op. cit., Mead.
4 Frank Field and Matthew Owen, *Beyond Punishment*, ICS, 1994, gives an overall view of how this debate has moved cyclically during the present century.
5 Welfare is here used as a shorthand to cover the basic means-tested income for those out of work. It currently sails under the banner of Income Support.
6 Turok I and Edge N, *The Jobs Gap in Britain's Cities*, Polity Press, 1999
7 Cited in *From Welfare to Work: Lessons from America*, edited by Alan Deacon, IEA, 1997.
8 This trend has been reinforced by tax and benefit

changes which give a privileged position to the single parent over the married couple. It is in this way that the welfare system sends out strong messages about behaviour; and the populace, being rational, pick up the vibes quickly.

9 The number of single parents on benefit has begun to fall, but this fall was recorded only after the number of jobs in the economy began to increase. The movement out of the current recession was first apparent in Scotland, and it is not without significance that the number of single parents claiming benefit began to fall first in this area.

10 The scheme is nevertheless important in changing the ethos of welfare from one of passive receipt to one of greater reciprocity of duties; of the state to provide benefit and the claimant to be an active working citizen as soon as that becomes a possibility.

11 i.e. Families where there are a series of boyfriends resulting in a number of children by different fathers.

10. Two Contrary Views on Welfare Reform*

Two views about the future of welfare are now before the country. Our view is set out in the Government's Green Paper on welfare reform, *New Ambitions for Our Country: A New Contract for Welfare*. Here welfare is seen as an inclusive agent and one which increasingly should be based on the idea of contract. Welfare costs should be much more clearly marked and who picks up the price tag made much more transparent. Transfers to the poor should be clearly identified as support gained from taxpayers by an appeal to altruism and as a reward for good citizenship. One assumption upon which the Green Paper was written was that only by building up insurance based welfare, with entitlement based on contributions, would it be possible to maintain universal provision.

A contrasting vision is presented by the emerging tax credit system. It is now clear that the Working Families Tax Credit (WFTC) is not a one-off initiative, but the start of the most major recasting of the welfare state for people of working age. A Disabled Persons Tax Credit is in place and the Child Care Tax Credits are already part of both the Disabled Persons' and Working Families' Tax Credits. Persistent leaks in the media suggest the Government would like to abolish Housing Benefit and Council Tax Benefit for non-retired claimants, replacing these benefits with a Housing Tax Credit.

The scheme is nothing if not ambitious. A single-earner couple with two children under 11, for example, could be still receiving WFTC with earnings up to around £370 per week. This is just over 90 per cent of the average earnings of all full-time adult employees. Relevant childcare costs and/or different family composition could push this figure even higher.

The Select Committee cannot now sensibly view the future and potential of national insurance without also considering the emerging tax credit system.

There is a fundamental division between these two approaches to reform which centres on how each group sees welfare functioning, particularly how welfare impacts on human behaviour. Tax Credits are old wine in new bottles. Despite the change in name the Credits are a means-tested benefit. As with all means tests they penalise success. Under the Tax Credits system the lower a person's income (at least for the purposes of filling in the claim form) the higher will be the taxpayers' subsidy. The opposite is also true. Gaining higher incomes will be rewarded by a lower credit.

For millions of people low-paid jobs are the only option currently open to them. But in deciding how to assist this group should the overwhelming drive be to reward only on the basis that people stay on low income? Should we provide financial disincentives for people who work harder and raise their income? Is failure an outcome which Governments should subsidise? And the use of the word subsidy in this context is right, for the tax credit will be paid from general taxation, and not by contributions.[1] While some people will be on low income, and will rightly gain help, the whole emphasis of this approach to welfare changes is to penalise success.

The WFTC sees the reintroduction of the Speenhamland system of subsidising low wages. Employers are currently opposing running the tax credit, but it will not take long for even the dimmest amongst them to realise that the Government is offering them the right to draw upon large sums of taxpayers' money to subsidise the wages bill.

Soon there will be few jobs advertised paying less than £200 per week – the guaranteed minimum income the Treasury claims for the Working Families Tax Credit. Employees enquiring for work will be offered first the WFTC application form. Employers will increasingly pay only the minimum wage at £3.60 an hour and draw the rest of the £200 wage from the Exchequer. Indeed, would it be sensible for them to do otherwise, given the system the Government is establishing?

For the millions of single workers earning above £3.60 an hour but less than £200 per week life will become tougher. Their wages will be squeezed twards £3.60. The alternative for some of them will be to boost wages by falsely claiming that they have a family. The Inland Revenue are responsible for checking the veracity of claims. Judging by the evidence given by the Inland Revenue to the Social Security Select Committee it looks as if the Inland Revenue will use similar anti-fraud measures as have been used for Family Credit. Regrettably the main benefit review of Family Credit was dropped by the Benefits Agency following the decision to transfer the benefit to the Inland Revenue.[2] The Working Families Tax Credit will attract large numbers of new claimants to a benefit of uncertain security.

The WFTC will push down wages. No employer will be able to offer a higher take-home pay for a wage between the minimum rate of £3.60 an hour and the £5 per hour guaranteed under the WFTC. The estimated bill for the tax credit will quickly soar, while the distribution of earnings towards the bottom end of the scale will take a marked downward shift. The only plus for the scheme is that currently the WFTC is available only to those with children, although a pilot for childless couples is being run. Childless people will find it harder to gain work for they cannot be offered the new weekly £200 minimum wage.

The minimum wage has been a success beyond all expectations. Wages have increased for the lowest paid without unemployment rising. Surely the approach should be to operate on this success and begin a review of the minimum wage. For the reasons I have just given, the advent of Tax Credits now largely undermines any future gains which could come from increasing the minimum wage.

A full-blown tax credit system cannot survive in the longer run. Without any contribution-based benefits the evil effects of means testing will become ever more disastrous. The only question is how long will taxpayers be prepared to foot an ever-escalating bill resulting from people naturally working the system and, to a lesser extent, from fraud.

Notes

* Evidence given to the Social Security Select Committee's inquiry into the future of the national insurance system, 3 November, 1999.
1. The funding of the WFTC through general taxation contrasts sharply with the transparency of contribution and entitlement which is so central to *New Ambitions for Our Country: A New Contract for Welfare*.
2. While I held the counter-fraud brief as Minister I ordered that this benefit review should be carried out. This decision was countermanded following my resignation.

11. A Year of Delivery*

Britain is experiencing a sustained period of economic prosperity unlike other times during this century. A record number of people in work is both a cause for rising prosperity and a sign of structural changes. This rise in prosperity is accompanied by a collapse in the way life is lived by a minority of the poor. Here a combination of persistent unemployment and drink and drugs is giving rise to a new barbarism. These rapidly collapsing social conditions make reforming welfare along the lines of encouraging work, rewarding savings and enhancing honesty more, not less, important. While the tax credit system, which is fast becoming a major welfare player, offers immediate advantages to people moving from benefit to work, it is simultaneously sowing the seeds of further social destruction. It will undermine still further those verities which welfare should reinforce. The repositioning of welfare on a contract or insurance basis, as promised in the Welfare Reform Green Paper, becomes more urgent.

Economic change
What is happening in the economy isn't simply a question that, for most people, life is ever easier and more interesting. That is undeniably true. Real incomes continue to rise and, despite two major recessions in the early 1980s and the 1990s, more people are in work. The two and a half million

additional jobs over and above those registered in 1979 are one of the very reasons why life has never been better for the vast majority of people. There is now a record number of people in work.

This good news is itself a reflection of much more substantial changes in the working of our economy which rarely surface in public discussions. In some important respects our country now has a number of key economic strengths which characterised the British economy prior to 1914. Our major overseas investments were subsequently dissipated by the costs of two world wars. However, we once again have very substantial overseas holdings. We are a rentier country again with 32 per cent of our balance of payments recording transfer incomes coming back into this country.

A second strength is the breaking of the wage push inflationary cycle. One of the best introductions to this economic change of gear comes in a recent lecture by DeAnne Julius.[1] Our open door trade policy has resulted in the British consumer being the beneficiary of stable or falling prices. A growing share of our trade is in what is called the global market, where inflation has most clearly been tamed. When prices rises do occur they are more likely to be caused by a worldwide product shortage than from the traditional wage push inflation which characterised so much of the post-war period in Britain.

But this record of success is only part, although thankfully a very large part, of the story. A major economic advance for the majority is taking place in parallel with the near-collapse of civilised life for those at the very bottom of our society.

Life at the bottom

Some people have a romantic view of poverty. That has never been my stance. Poverty is loathsome. It tests, and in the process, all too often destroys the best of human qualities. But while poverty is very much part of what I wish to describe, it is only *part* of the story. It is the behaviour of some of the poor who have been plunged to the depths by the cruellest of combinations – idleness born of a generation of unemployment and an increasing dependence upon drink and drugs. It is this most deadly of cocktails which is causing such havoc in our inner city areas.

Children in such families often have no idea what a parent's love is. For all too many of these parents, their children are no more than a lodger who shares the same dwelling and whose main value is as a passport to a benefit book. These parents seem incapable of that most basic of parental feelings where a child's interests is put before their own.

The children turn up to school scruffy. They are hungry. Inadequate free school meals are their main food of the day. Some children disappear for weeks on end and then reappear after sleeping rough, or bedding down on a friend's floor. What is the difference between this life, and those lucky enough to experience being fostered? Often, the distinction is that there is food in the cupboard for those lucky enough to be taken away from their parents, even for a short period.

Children go home not knowing if they are to be let in, or if there will be anyone there to do the letting in. The lives of these poor children are in chaos. It is hardly surprising that their behaviour all too often reflects that disorder.

Gangs of youths maraud around drinking, presenting a threatening presence. Areas are colonised as the gang stakes out its territory against other groups with an off-licence all too often acting as the assembly of these mini city states.

A new barbarism stalks the poorest areas. Behaviour which would have been as exceptional as it was unacceptable is fast becoming the norm. The life of the decent poor who live cheek by jowl with these events is becoming less and less tolerable.

For many of the poor who man the front line in this fight against disorder their home is no longer a castle, although many of this group wish that it was in the original mediaeval sense of the term. Garden walls are kicked down. Windows rattle from the balls which are constantly kicked at them. There is the nightmare of the laughing faces as a severely disabled person is taken out for a walk. No one knows when the noise will quell so that some sleep can be snatched.

Decent families feel that a new kind of warfare is being waged all around them. And, let me again stress, many of these decent families attempting to hold the line against this social anarchy are themselves poor. Many others are in straightened circumstances. Their standards of honour, of working, of saving, of bringing up their children as good citizens, are mocked and attacked from all quarters.

Public officials seem paralysed when the cry goes up for help. The police are so over-stretched that no amount of efficient working will deliver the degree of protection that is required. Hard-earned wages are taxed to pay benefits to people who roll around on drink or drugs. It would be bad enough if such people wallowed in their own self-inflicted misery. But they smash their way into the lives of decent citizens bringing destruction in their wake.

Such is the life experienced by those decent citizens who, through lack of choice, hold the front line against this new barbarism. They know that there is no simple panacea which will cure such evils. But they question why it is that hardly any youth custody orders have been imposed 12 months after the Act giving such power to local authorities came into force. Likewise, they puzzle why they should be called upon to pay the housing benefit for neighbours whose behaviour is more akin to life in the jungle. Should not such families be evicted, and refused rehousing until they start to behave themselves? If such people have children why aren't the children taken into care while their parents ponder what it is like not to have any neighbours to terrorise? These are just a few questions raised by those very families who are holding out against Britain's new barbarism.

Again I stress to the point of boredom that I am not here generalising about all those who are poor, or, even the majority of poor. The group to which I have tried to focus your attention is small, even in a poor area. But the impact of the behaviour of this small group is out of all proportion to its size, and the size of this group is growing. Loutism is seen to pay and successful loutism breeds even more crude behaviour.

While this barbarism is only one of the many issues which has to be considered as a factor influencing welfare reform, it is a crucial one. In an age when Christianity has ever less force in moulding human behaviour, the role welfare can play in helping shape behaviour should be a prime consideration in the design of welfare reform.

Fundamental reform

So to my second theme. Fundamental welfare reform is taking place, but anyone could be forgiven for thinking otherwise. The Welfare Reform and Pensions Act attracted much attention. As a bill it survived only under the protection of the Government's 179 majority over all other parties. On many key decisions the Government, marshalling its forces on a three line whip, could only persuade a minority of the House of Commons to go into the division lobby on its side. The Government experienced difficulties with this measure largely because it flew in the face of the lodestars of encouraging work, savings and honesty by which it had committed itself to reform welfare.

While there are some small, important changes which will be effected by the Act, there is nothing to distinguish the thrust of the second half of the Act from previous Tory cut measures which masqueraded as reforms. Belief in the beneficial effects of stakeholder pension proposals, which occupy the first part of the Act, is, sadly, an example of where the hope of well-wishers flies in the face of experience and even logic.

While the Government was involved in trench warfare with all too many of its supporters in attempting to drag the Welfare Reform and Pensions Bill on to the statute book, measures which amounted to a genuine welfare reform glided down the legislative ship-way. Any doubts MPs expressed were overwhelmed by the cheering of Government supporters at the launch of these genuine welfare reform measures. As I will shortly register my fears about where this welfare reform programme will lead the country

I wish to begin by commending the Chancellor on the drive, skills and determination he displays in making a reality of his vision of welfare reform. Politically he resembles an Olympic athlete, at the peak of his powers.

In case you have not guessed the programme which I believe deserves a billing as welfare reform, let me end your suspense. I am talking about the tax credit system which is fast being assembled and brought into play. It is now clear that the introduction of the Working Families Tax Credit is not an aberration. To what might have been seen as a move to ensure that a person moving from benefit into work was financially better off – an objective on which practically the whole country is agreed – the tax credit system already has taken on a far more substantial appearance. Child care credits were always an important part of the original strategy. But a disabled person's tax credit has since been announced, and the spin doctors have been whizzing here there and everywhere with suggestions that housing benefit has been moved onto death row. It will be replaced by a Housing Tax Credit.

Moreover, the new tax credit system covers people who would not normally be beneficiaries of means tested assistance. Tax credit eligibility sweeps up the income scale. The scheme is nothing if not ambitious. A single-earner couple with 2 children under 11, for example, could be still be receiving WFTC with earnings up to around £370 per week. This is just over 90 per cent of the average earnings of all full-time adult employees. Relevant childcare costs and/or different family composition push this figure even higher.

The developing strategy is deployed with dazzling skill. And besides, is it possible to argue against any of these moves if they are considered individually? Indeed, even when such single moves are linked with the awarding of a child care tax credit, it is still well nigh impossible to get a questioning discussion off the ground. Are we not in favour of as many people with disabilities working who wish to work? And how many people need convincing that housing benefit is now part of the problem as well as the cure?

It is not on any one of these initiatives that attention should be directed. It is, rather, the principle which underpins tax credit which needs the searchlight of public debate focused upon it. It is also the strategy underpinning the raft of tax credit reforms which similarly needs to become part of the public debate.

The central idea behind a tax credit system is nothing if not simple. It is to establish a minimum income and to do so without offering help to all and sundry, irrespective of their financial circumstances. Only those people with incomes below a certain level will be helped. Simple, yes, but noble too. There is no doubt that the advocates of a tax credit system are driven by the highest of motives. But to adapt Edith Carvell's phrase that patriotism alone is not enough, are high motives alone a secure enough basis for policy, particularly when the ambitions for the tax credit system has yet to be fully unveiled?

Tax credits are being marketed as a new product. But are not tax credits simply a new means-tested benefit branded under a new name? Just how substantial are the differences claimed for this new initiative? The Working Family Tax Credit replaces Family Credit. While the Family Credit was clearly a benefit, the Government claims that the Working

Family Tax Credit is part of the wage and tax system. But to what does this difference amount? Once behind the rhetoric, how does that statement look?

The WFTC is the child of Family Credit. The Family Credit staff at Preston have been moved lock stock and barrel to become an important outpost of the Treasury's expanding empire.

How significant is the Treasury claim that the payment of WFTC in the wage packet is a decisive change which will lead to a similar change in the attitude of benefit recipients to what would otherwise be an unacceptably low paid job?

It is undoubtedly true that there are many people who work but who are only marginally financially better off by doing so. There are others who, once work expenses have been taken into account, are actually worse off. Some – many perhaps – of this group continue to work what are euphemistically called 'unsocial' hours; a 4.30 to 5.00 am start, for example, to travel many miles to begin a 6 am shift. The Chancellor is right in his wish to salute this group who uphold the importance of work by making the income gap between benefit and work larger than it is at present.

But that goal would have been just as easily achieved by making Family Credit more generous, by increasing the eligibility threshold, or by lowering the clawback, or by introducing a child care component, or by all or any combination of these moves. The Chancellor argues that by putting the credit into the wage packet the incentive to work is increased compared to a benefit payment made to workers on low pay, and, in so doing, strikes another blow against welfare dependency.

This argument cannot hold for people on benefit and testing the job market to see what their rewards will be. The information crucial to any of these decisions is the net take home pay over and above the benefit income. How that sum is paid is immaterial. There is no consumer preference to be expressed for, as yet, there is no wage packet through which the credit is paid. The individual relies either on benefit advice from the Jobcentre, a welfare rights agency, or simply guesses what their income may be. At this stage no one questions the mechanism by which any top-up will be paid.

It may be that, once in work, individuals prefer to have all their rewards paid through the wage packet. But again, pause, and think what is being asserted. We are all told that low paid jobs in particular are notoriously insecure. Jobs come and go and workers are left jumping from one position to another in order to survive. Low paid jobs have far less trade union cover. It is therefore easier for employers so minded to bully workers in all kinds of disturbing ways.

Which is the more secure position? To apply to the Inland Revenue to continue to claim WFTC, which is the procedure for a person between jobs, with all the delays this will inevitably entail? Or to know that, whatever happens, the incentive to take a low paid jobs whether that subsidy is called a Family Credit or a WFTC, will continue to be paid via a bank or a post office until a new claim has been registered?

Consider for a moment how vulnerable a single parent, or a single wage household, is in these circumstances. Once a job is lost they become dependent on the goodwill of their ex-employer, whom they may have left after a dispute, to continue paying the WFTC. Under family credit payments of benefit continue to arrive at the bank account, or be ready to be picked up at the post office. The great irony is that only where two parents in work are involved has the Government offered any choice, and this choice is only over who should receive the credit.

It is surely the size of the gap between benefit and work which is crucial, with the means of delivering the work incentive a secondary consideration. Not so long ago I was talking to a single mother in my local surgery. During our conversation she questioned her entitlement under what would soon be the WFTC. I was careful to dress up my reply in the Treasury garb, emphasising that the wage supplement was a tax credit. A look of pity spread over her young face. Her hand came across the desk and was put on my arm. 'Just stick to emphasising how much it is worth. The name will not pay any bills.' Feel the width, and don't worry about the name, is good advice for politicians to follow.

There are distinct public accounting differences between a credit and a benefit, but isn't the issue again one of style, rather than substance? A credit appears like a tax allowance, as a loss of revenue. Family Credit appeared as a benefit, and as part of the welfare bill. A tax credit does not appear as part of those accounts showing the size of Government expenditure. A benefit like the Family Credit does. But isn't it true that, pound for pound, a tax credit and a family credit cost equal amounts to the taxpayer?

All means-tests reward failure. All means-tests penalise success. Any modern system of welfare will rely, to some extent, on a means-tested approach. But because any means-tested system is essentially about rewarding failure and penalising success, most observers argue for means-tests to be as constrained as possible. Few argue for their extension.

That is precisely what the tax credit system does. And a question I leave with you is whether the tax credit system fast being assembled will turn out to be a cuckoo's egg neatly laid in the national insurance nest.

An alternative

So to my third and last theme. The National Insurance system stands in contra distinction to tax credits. It promotes different values, it has a different view to tax credits on how welfare interacts with human character. Beveridge, after surveying the attitudes and opinions during the darkest period of the Second World War concluded that the contributory principle should be the rock on which the new social security system should be built. In his report he categorised what he saw as the reasons why insurance was to be preferred over other systems of social security:[2]

- the insured person themselves 'can pay and like to pay and would rather pay than not do so';
- by paying contributions 'citizens as insured persons realised they cannot get more than certain benefits for certain contributions';
- the contributions 'provides automatically the record by which insured persons' claims for benefit can be judged.

To these three advantages of how insurance works with

the grain of human nature, at least as far as the British understand the issue, Beveridge cited other advantages, the most important of which was the pooling of risk which most people face at one time or another during their lives. A national insurance scheme, at one and the same time, prevents the private sector cherrypicking the best customers and thereby leaving taxpayers to pick up the bills for those whom the private market rejects. Average costs are therefore lower than they would otherwise be.

These advantages, or attractions to voters of national insurance, remain active forces in the economic and political debate. But they are not the only attractions to today's electorate. I would suggest that, in addition, there are four other major advantages which takes the insurance scheme into the millennium. Let me briefly list them.

- National insurance reaffirms the state's duty to enforce an acceptable minimum. I say state deliberately. I do not mean Government. The state is the body to which all other bodies in political society owe allegiance, and while Governments are usually by far and away the most powerful of such organisations, they are not the state. By referring to the state enforcing a minimum discussion is about how public and private partnerships can achieve this end.
- This leads to the second of national insurance's current advantages in that the national minimum can in some circumstances be achieved only by such a partnership, but without the Government's participation, that minimum will in some instances prove all too elusive.

Moreover, while the minimum may be enforced by a combined public and private action, the role of the Government, as opposed to other bodies, is concerned only with that minimum provision. It is not a legitimate role for Government, in my opinion, to force people, for example, to save for a pension other than one which gives a minimum level of coverage, i.e. lifts the recipient free of means-testing. A higher pension is a desirable objective, but individuals should decide for themselves how much extra pension provision over the minimum they would like. Private companies, and public bodies like mutual societies, have a legitimate role in trying to convince individuals that they should save more than the minimum. To repeat: that is not a legitimate role for Government.

- We live in an age where voters demand lower taxes. National insurance is not seen as a tax, despite the Government now regularly referring to it as such. It is therefore possible to provide the minimum income which any civilised society needs to offer without pushing up taxes. So strong is the tide against raising taxes that it will not be long before the Government opens up discussions on financing the NHS through a national insurance type system.
- The final attraction of national insurance in the new millennium is one which will grow ever more important as it links directly to the collapse of decent behaviour amongst the minority of poor. Indeed, I wish to suggest that the behaviour of this group is so reprehensible, and so opposed by the poor themselves, that the group to

which I refer is best described as an underclass. The need to move the behaviour of this group in a more civilised direction – which by definition if successful will see the individuals and families exit themselves from the underclass – is an issue/matter which will move sharply up the political agenda.

In what ways can welfare be used to help shape public behaviour in a more acceptable direction? There are three initiatives which should be taken. Welfare reform by itself offers no panacea in countering the significant changes in the public's behaviour which are apparent throughout society, and seem more exaggerated in some of the poorest inner city areas. Reforms which the Home Secretary has already piloted on to the Statute Book (with more in the pipeline) are setting a new framework of civil and criminal sanctions. These new powers aim at tilting the balance in favour of public order, for example, by the use of youth curfews. Without this new framework, welfare changes would have less impact on behaviour. But combined with the Home Secretary's overall strategy, key welfare changes can have a much greater impact than could be hoped for as initiatives in their own right.

For the children in the underclass the one place which offers immediate care and long-term hope is the school. Schools generally provide the one area of stability in the lives of these children. But they can only offer this stability if children attend. It is on this issue that teachers believe the Social Exclusion Unit have failed to make a clear enough distinction between children who miss school without the permission or knowledge of their parents, and those children who go missing for more often for long periods of time, whose parents couldn't care what their children are doing, or who are actively in connivance with them in their absence.

The Home Office is suggesting fining parents up to £5,000 as children fail to turn up to school regularly. In Birkenhead the courts might as well levy a £5 million fine. These sums make no sense to the parents we are talking about who live all too often a hand to mouth existence.

What these parents do care about is the benefit book.[3] For too many of them the value of their children lies in the passport to benefit which those children provide. The loss of the benefit book, especially child benefit, is a sanction which should be employed. Drawing child benefit should become conditional on a satisfactory school attendance record.

Moreover, schools should be pivotal in triggering this decision. This change would need to be worked out fully with, for example, the school staff being protected against the rage of some parents who lose this source of income. But this move should be seen as the first of a series of reforms – such as the delivery of children's social services – which begin to give schools the powers equivalent to the responsibilities which now rest upon them.

The second series of reforms concern national insurance. The Government's welfare reform green paper was deliberately entitled *A New Contract for Welfare*. This title was chosen to signify that welfare would be reformed along the lines of a clear contract. Contributions would be paid and the returned benefits would be guaranteed on the basis of those earmarked payments.

A contract basis upon which to reform welfare was decided upon for a number of reasons. It was adopted, in part, in realisation of the rock and hard place in which politicians find themselves – a resistance by voters to tax increases while at the same time the very same voters are demanding improvements in public services. Lloyd George saw insurance as a way round this dilemma. So too did the authors of the Green Paper.

But the insurance contract approach was also adopted because of its centrality to the Government's programme to duties and responsibilities. It was felt, rightly in my view, that the link between drawing benefit and the payment of those benefits had been weakened, particularly amongst younger people. Insurance benefits gave coverage for basic needs and did so with a price tag attached. There was no bottomless financial pit from which funds could come to finance welfare. Insurance helps teach the simple fact that benefits have to be paid for. More could of course be achieved on this front. The Social Security Select Committee in the last parliament recommended issuing insurance statements annually giving details of pension rights being built up, benefits claimed during the year, as well as details of the sum of contributions paid into the scheme. As well as giving a greater sense of ownership to the scheme, such statements would help in the fight against the piggybacking of national insurance numbers which is a technique used by gangs to fraudulently claim often large sums of money.

The insurance contract principle was adopted in the green paper for the impact it would have in helping mould the public culture within which people stake out their own private lives. In place of what the Prime Minister described as the something for nothing society, contract welfare would help strengthen the importance of personal pride which grows as people know what is expected of them and as they meet those expectations. Public culture, like elephants, are notoriously difficult to describe, but, also like elephants, can make their presence felt.

It is difficult to see how a tax credit system which grows in importance with practically every welfare announcement, fits in with this strategy. Indeed it directly challenges it. As do the cuts in national insurance benefits which were a marked feature of the recent Welfare Reform and Pensions Act.

The tax credit system sends out a message which conflicts with that emanating from an insurance based welfare. Tax credits help poor people now, and that is an important objective. One danger of this approach, however, is that a temporary expedient becomes all too quickly part of the established order. The Conservative Government in 1971 introduced the Family Income Supplement (introduced in place of fulfilling its election pledge to increase family allowances, as they were then called). FIS was then puffed up into the Family Credit, and that benefit, as we have already seen, now sails under the Working Families Tax Credit colours.

The legitimate objective of meeting the needs of the poor now, because the measure become permanent, began to strengthen anti-social behaviour. As with all means-tested benefits FIS, Family Credit, and the Working Families Tax Credit, penalise those who work harder, those who save, and those who tell the truth.

There is little point in suggesting a Government rethink on its tax credit strategy. Governments simply do not work like that. What could be expected however is a serious questioning of where the tax credit system will lead. And, hopefully, as a result of that discussion, an agreement to freeze tax credit eligibility levels. That would allow a subsequent revision of the minimum wage, together with rises in real income, floating the poor off tax credits. Not to adopt such a strategy will bring forth a position we now find ourselves in respect to housing benefit, although magnified many times over. The housing benefit bill rises now largely because rents rise. The benefit system has therefore become part of the problem, not its solution. So too with tax credits. Wages will be pushed towards the minimum. More and more employers will see the benefit as a major new subsidy enhancing their profitability. The process then becomes accumulative, with all the obvious consequences in costs to the taxpayer.

Conclusion

Britain is experiencing a sustained period of economic prosperity unlike other times during this century. A record number of people in work is both a cause for rising prosperity and a sign of structural changes. This rise in prosperity is accompanied by a collapse in the way life is lived by a minority of the poor. Here a combination of persistent unemployment and drink and drugs is giving rise to a new barbarism. These rapidly collapsing social conditions make reforming welfare along the lines of encouraging work, rewarding savings and enhancing honesty more not less important. While the tax credit system, which is fast becoming a major welfare player, offers immediate advantages to people moving from benefit to work, it is simultaneously sowing the seeds of further social destruction. It will undermine still further those verities which welfare should reinforce. The repositioning of welfare on a contract or insurance basis, as promised in the Welfare Reform Green Paper, becomes more urgent.

Notes

★ Lecture given to Politiea on 23 November, 1999.
1 DeAnne Julius, Back to the Future of Low Global Inflation, a lecture given at the University of Birmingham, 20 October 1999.
2 Sir William Beveridge, Social Insurance and Allied Services, HMSO, 1942, paragraph 274.
3 For a discussion on conditionality rules for benefit see Frank Field and Matthew Owen, *Beyond Punishment*, ICS, 1994.

Publications

SMF Papers

1. *The Social Market Economy*
   Robert Skidelsky
   1989   £3.50

2. *Responses to Robert Skidelsky on the Social Market Economy*
   Sarah Benton, Kurt Biedenkopf, Frank Field, Danny Finkelstein, Francis Hawkings, Graham Mather
   1989   £3.50

3. *Europe Without Currency Barriers*
   Samuel Brittan, Michael Artis
   1989   £5.00

4. *Greening the White Paper: A Strategy for NHS Reform*
   Gwyn Bevan, Marshall Marinker
   1989   £2.00

5. *Education and the Labour Market: An English Disaster*
   Adrian Wooldridge
   1990   £5.00

6. *Crisis in Eastern Europe: Roots and Prospects*
   Robin Okey
   1990   £4.00

7. *Fighting Fiscal Privilege: Towards a Fiscal Constitution*
   Deepak Lal
   1990   £4.00

8. *Eastern Europe in Transition*
   Clive Crook, Daniel Franklin
   1990   £5.00

9. *The Open Network and its Enemies: Towards a Contestable Telecommunications Market*
   Danny Finkelstein, Craig Arnall
   1990   £2.00

10. *A Restatement of Economic Liberalism*
    Samuel Brittan
    1990   £5.00

11. *Standards in Schools: Assessment, Accountability and the Purposes of Education*
    John Marks
    1991   £6.00

12. *Deeper Share Ownership*
    Matthew Gaved, Anthony Goodman
    1992   £3.00

13. *Fighting Leviathan: Building Social Markets that Work*
    Howard Davies
    1992   £6.00

14. *The Age of Entitlement*
    David Willetts
    1993   £6.00

15. *Schools and the State*
    Evan Davis
    1993   £6.00

16. *Public Sector Pay: In Search of Sanity*
    Ron Beadle
    1993   £4.00

17. *Beyond Next Steps: a Civil Service for the 1990s*
    Sir Peter Kemp
    1993   £4.00

18. *Post-Communist Societies in Transition: A Social Market Perspective*
    John Gray
    1994   £4.00

19. *Two Cheers for the Institutions*
    Stanley Wright
    1994   £5.00

20. *Civic Conservatism*
    David Willetts
    1994   £5.00

21. *The Undoing of Conservatism*
    John Gray
    1994   £5.00

22. *Meritocracy and the 'Classless Society'*
    Adrian Wooldridge
    1995   £8.00

23. *Public Spending into the Millennium*
    Nick Bosanquet
    1995   £5.00

24. *Communities in the Countryside*
    Damian Green
    1996   £10.00

25. *The Ties that Bind Us*
    Matthew d'Ancona
    1996   £10.00

26. *The Prospects for Public Spending*
    Andrew Tyrie
    1996   £7.50

27. *Taxing and Spending Dilemmas*
    Norman Gemmell
    1997   £10.00

28. *Making Shoplifters Pay: Retail Civil Recovery*
    Joshua Bamfield
    1997   £12.00

29. *Britain's Relative Economic Decline 1870–1995: A Quantitative Perspective*
    Nicholas Crafts
    1997   £6.00

30. *Beyond the Welfare State*
    Robert Skidelsky
    1997   £8.00

31. *Lessons from the Republicans*
    Tim Hames and Alan Grant
    1997   £12.00

32. *Reforming Welfare*
    Frank Field
    1997   £5.00

33. *Dilemmas in Modern Health Care*
    ed. John Spiers
    1997   £10.00

34. *Ready for Treatment*
    Nick Bosanquet and Stephen Pollard
    1997   £5.00

35. *The Future of Welfare*
    ed. Roderick Nye
    1998   £10.00

36. *Welfare to Work*
    David Willetts
    1998   £10.00

37. *Back on Target*
    Nick Bosanquet and Tony Hockley
    1998   £10.00

38. *The State of the Future*
Robert Skidelsky, Walter Eltis,
Evan Davis, Norman Gemmell,
Meghnad Desai
1998 £10.00

39. *Reflections on Welfare Reform*
Frank Field
1998 £10.00

40. *The Purpose of Politics*
Oliver Letwin
1999 £8.00

41. *A Cue for Change*
Oliver Morgan
1999 £12.00

42. *The Social Market and the State*
edited by Alastair Kilmarnock
1999 £12.99

43. *A Question of Choice*
Stephen Pollard and
Katharine Raymond
1999 £10.00

44. *The Sex-Change Society*
Melanie Phillips
1999 £12.99

Reports

1. *Environment, Economics and Development after the 'Earth Summit'*
Andrew Cooper
1992 £3.00

2. *Another Great Depression? Historical Lessons for the 1990s*
Robert Skidelsky, Liam Halligan
1993 £5.00

3. *Exiting the Underclass: Policy towards America's Urban Poor*
Andrew Cooper,
Catherine Moylan
1993 £5.00

4. *Britain's Borrowing Problem*
Bill Robinson
1993 £5.00

Occasional Papers

1. *Deregulation*
David Willetts
1993 £3.00

2. *'There is No Such Thing as Society'*
Samuel Brittan
1993 £3.00

3. *The Opportunities for Private Funding in the NHS*
David Willetts
1993 £3.00

4. *A Social Market for Training*
Howard Davies
1993 £3.00

5. *Beyond Unemployment*
Robert Skidelsky, Liam Halligan
1993 £6.00

6. *Brighter Schools*
Michael Fallon
1993 £5.00

7. *Understanding 'Shock Therapy'*
   Jeffrey Sachs
   1994   £8.00

8. *Recruiting to the Little Platoons*
   William Waldegrave
   1994   £6.00

9. *The Culture of Anxiety: The Middle Class in Crisis*
   Matthew Symonds
   1994   £4.00

10. *What is left of Keynes?*
    Samuel Brittan, Meghnad Desai, Deepak Lal, Robert Skidelsky, Tom Wilson
    1994   £8.00

11. *Winning the Welfare Debate*
    Peter Lilley (Introduction by Frank Field)
    1995   £8.00

12. *Financing the Future of the Welfare State*
    Robert Skidelsky, Will Hutton
    1995   £5.00

13. *Picking Winners: The East Asian Experience*
    Ian Little
    1996   £8.00

14. *Over-the-Counter Medicines*
    Alan Maynard, Gerald Richardson
    1996   £5.00

15. *Pressure Group Politics in Modern Britain*
    Riddell, Waldegrave, Secrett, Bazalgette, Gaines, Parminter
    1996   £10.00

16. *Design Decisions: Improving the Public Effectiveness of Public Purchasing*
    Taylor, Fisher, Sorrell, Stephenson, Rawsthorn, Davis, Jenkins, Turner, Taylor
    1996   £5.00

17. *Stakeholding Society vs Enterprise Centre of Europe*
    Robert Skidelsky, Will Hutton
    1997   £3.00

18. *Setting Enterprise Free*
    Ian Lang
    1997   £3.00

19. *Community Values and the Market Economy*
    John Kay
    1997   £10.00

Other Papers

1. *Local Government and the Social Market*
   George Jones
   1991   £3.00

2. *Full Employment without Inflation*
   James Meade
   1994   £6.00

Memoranda/Discussion Papers

1. *Provider Choice: 'Opting In' through the Private Finance Initiative*
   Michael Fallon
   1993 £2.00

2. *The Importance of Resource Accounting*
   Evan Davis
   1993 £2.00

3. *Why There is No Time to Teach: What is wrong with the National Curriculum 10 Level Scale*
   John Marks
   1994 £5.00

4. *All Free Health Care Must be Effective*
   Brendan Devlin, Gwyn Bevan
   1994 £2.00

5. *Recruiting to the Little Platoons*
   William Waldegrave
   1994 £2.00

6. *Labour and the Public Services*
   John Willman
   1994 £5.00

7. *Organising Cost Effective Access to Justice*
   Gwyn Bevan, Tony Holland and Michael Partington
   1994 £5.00

8. *A Memo to Modernisers*
   Ron Beadle, Andrew Cooper, Evan Davis, Alex de Mont, Stephen Pollard, David Sainsbury, John Willman
   1994 £3.00

9. *Conservatives in Opposition: Republicans in the US*
   Daniel Finkelstein
   1994 £3.00

10. *Housing Benefit: Incentives for Reform*
    Greg Clark
    1994 £3.00

11. *The Market and Clause IV*
    Stephen Pollard
    1994 £1.00

12. *Yeltsin's Choice: Background to the Chechnya Crisis*
    Vladimir Mau
    1994 £3.00

13. *Teachers' Practices: A New Model for State Schools*
    Tony Meredith
    1994 £3.00

14. *The Right to Earn: Learning to Live with Top People's Pay*
    Ron Beadle
    1995 £5.00

15. *A Memo to Modernisers II*
    John Abbott, Peter Boone, Tom Chandos, Evan Davis, Alex de Mont, Ian Pearson, Stephen Pollard, Katharine Raymond, John Spiers
    1995 £3.00

16. *Schools, Selection and the Left*
    Stephen Pollard
    1995 £3.00

17. *The Future of Long-Term Care*
    Andrew Cooper, Roderick Nye
    1995 £3.00

18. *Better Job Options for Disabled People: Re-employ and Beyond*
Peter Thurnham
1995 £3.00

19. *Negative Equity and the Housing Market*
Andrew Cooper, Roderick Nye
1995 £1.00

20. *Industrial Injuries Compensation: Incentives to Change*
Dr Greg Clark, Iain Smedley
1995 £3.00

21. *Better Government by Design: Improving the Effectiveness of Public Purchasing*
Katharine Raymond, Marc Shaw
1996 £5.00

22. *A Memo to Modernisers III*
Evan Davis, John Kay, Alex de Mont, Stephen Pollard, Brian Pomeroy, Katharine Raymond
1996 £5.00

23. *The Citizen's Charter Five Years On*
Roderick Nye
1996 £3.00

24. *Standards of English and Maths in Primary Schools for 1995*
John Marks
1997 £10.00

25. *Standards of Reading, Spelling and Maths for 7-year-olds in Primary Schools for 1995*
John Marks
1997 £10.00

26. *An Expensive Lunch: The Political Economy of Britain's New Monetary Framework*
Robert Chote
1997 £3.00

27. *A Memo to Martin Taylor*
David Willetts
1997 £5.00

28. *Why Fundholding Should Stay*
David Colin-Thomé
1997 £2.00

29. *Lessons from Wisconsin's Welfare Reform*
J. Jean Rogers
1997 £5.00

30. *The Sex-Change State*
Melanie Phillips
1997 £4.00

31. *Freedom and the Family*
William Hague
1998 £3.00

32. *Practical Road Pricing*
Stephen Glaister
1998 £5.00

33. *Education Action Zones: The Conditions of Success*
Robert Skidelsky and Katharine Raymond
1998 £8.00

34. *New Dynamics in Public Health Policy*
Nick Bosanquet and Tony Hockley
1998 £5.00

35. *An Anatomy of Failure: Standards in English Schools for 1997*
John Marks
1998 £10.00

36. *Beyond the PSBR: Auditing the New Public Finances*
Evan Davis and Brian Pomeroy
1998 £3.00

37. *Wanted: A New Consumer Affairs Strategy*
Mark Boléat
1999 £10.00

38. *A Fruitless Marriage? Same-sex Couples and Partnership Rights*
Evan Davis and Melanie Phillips
1999 £5.00

Trident Trust/ SMF Contributions to Policy

1. *Welfare to Work: The* America Works *Experience*
Roderick Nye (Introduction by John Spiers)
1996 £5.00

2. *Job Insecurity vs Labour Market Flexibility*
David Smith (Introduction by John Spiers)
1997 £5.00

3. *How Effective is Work Experience?*
Greg Clark and Katharine Raymond (Foreword by Colin Cooke-Priest)
1997 £4.00

Hard Data

1. *The Rowntree Inquiry and 'Trickle Down'*
Andrew Cooper, Roderick Nye
1995 £1.00

2. *Costing the Public Policy Agenda: A week of the* Today *Programme*
Andrew Cooper
1995 not available

3. *Universal Nursery Education and Playgroups*
Andrew Cooper, Roderick Nye
1995 £2.00

4. *Social Security Costs of the Social Chapter*
Andrew Cooper, Marc Shaw
1995 £1.00

5. *What Price a Life?*
Andrew Cooper, Roderick Nye
1995 £1.00

Centre for Post-Collectivist Studies

1. *Russia's Stormy Path to Reform*
   Robert Skidelsky (ed.)
   1995 £6.00

2. *Macroeconomic Stabilisation in Russia: Lessons of Reforms, 1992–1995*
   Robert Skidelsky, Liam Halligan
   1996 £5.00

3. *The End of Order*
   Francis Fukuyama
   1997 £9.50

4. *From Socialism to Capitalism: What is meant by the 'Change of System'?*
   János Kornai
   1998 £8.00

5. *The Politics of Economic Reform*
   Robert Skidelsky (ed.)
   1998 £12.00

6. *The Rise and Fall of the Swedish Model*
   Mauricio Rojas
   1998 £10.00

7. *Capital Regulation: For and Against*
   Robert Skidelsky, Nigel Lawson, John Flemming, Meghnad Desai, Paul Davidson
   1999 £5.00

8. *Russia: the 1998 Crisis and Beyond*
   Kalin Nikolov
   1999 £5.00

9. *Welfare After Communism*
   János Kornai
   1999 £6.00

10. *Financial Crises*
    Robert Skidelsky (ed.)
    2000 £9.50

11. *Killing Development: Money Laundering in the Global Economy*
    Alan Jones, Barry Rider, Graham Saltmarsh, Louise Shelley
    2000 £6.00

Stockholm Network

1. *Millennium Doom*
   Mauricio Rojas
   1999 £10.00

2. *A European Harmony?*
   Kurt Wickman, Philippe Manière, David Smith, Gunnar Uldall
   1999 £6.00

Briefings

1. *A Guide to Russia's Parliamentary Elections*
   Liam Halligan,
   Boris Mozdoukhov
   1995   £10.00

SMF/Profile Books

1. *Is Conservatism Dead?*
   John Gray and David Willetts
   1997   £8.99

2. *A Better State of Health*
   John Willman
   1998   £8.99

3. *Will Europe Work?*
   David Smith
   1999   £8.99